To Monique & Alfred,

a little souvenir of England

from Simone & Alan.

September 1974.

ENGLISH CATHEDRALS in colour

1   *Carlisle: Renaissance woodwork, c. 1542*

2   *(overleaf) Durham: the sanctuary knocker*

BRYAN LITTLE

English
Cathedrals

in colour

photographs by A. F. Kersting

B. T. BATSFORD, London

Books by Bryan Little

The Building of Bath
Cheltenham
The Three Choirs Cities
Exeter
The City and County of Bristol
The Life and Work of James Gibbs
Portrait of Cambridge
   (with A. F. Kersting as photographer)
The Monmouth Episode

Crusoe's Captain
Cambridge Discovered
Bath Portrait
English Historic Architecture
Catholic Churches Since 1623
Cheltenham in Pictures
Portrait of Somerset
Birmingham Buildings

First published 1972
Text © Bryan Little 1972
Photographs © A. F. Kersting 1972

Filmset by Keyspools Ltd., Golborne, Lancs.
Printed and bound in Great Britain
by C. Tinling & Co. Ltd., London and Prescot,
for the publishers B. T. Batsford Ltd.,
4 Fitzhardinge Street, WIH OAH

Contents

3   Ripon: from a stall end, sixteenth century

List of illustrations

Foreword

The literature of England's cathedrals is already vast. But new insights into their history, and into their fabrics as these have been conditioned by liturgical needs and by the money available to bishops and their clergy, constantly come with changes in our social and religious outlook. So a new book on this country's cathedrals, of ancient foundation or newer status, of the Established Church or the Roman Catholic minority, can still find a good place along with those compiled since the days of the Georgian antiquarians and slightly later architectural students. In my short introduction, largely based on what I have told University extra-mural classes in Bath and elsewhere, I have tried to restate, factually and with clarity, the nature, the basic history, the financial conditioning and the post-Reformation vicissitudes of the churches which have, for varying periods, contained the thrones of the bishops who have, since Anglo-Saxon times, presided over England's episcopal Churches. I have dealt with bishops and their dioceses, with their thrones and tombs, and with choirs and sanctuaries rather than with less essential, though often impressive naves which are now again coming into their own as worshipping places, regularly or on special occasions, of the laity. I mention the 'parish church' and the Roman Catholic cathedrals, and glance briefly at their position in a society in which the place of organised religion is very different from that which prevailed before the Reformation.

In my short essays on the twenty-six 'traditionally cathedralesque' cathedrals I deal with their history, their main architectural evolution, and with some of their furnishings. I also bring out the point that *every* one of them has *some* point in which it is unique or excels all others.

B.D.G.L.
Bristol, January, 1972

The Background

HISTORY, WORSHIP AND FINANCE

The splendid parish church at Patrington in the East Riding of Yorkshire is sometimes called 'The Cathedral of Holderness'. The same title, with Romney Marsh as its supposed diocese, has been applied to the fine Kentish church at Lydd. The noble church at Newland in Gloucestershire has been called 'The Cathedral' of the Forest of Dean. The same title, with less justification, has been applied to the well-towered church at Widecombe in Dartmoor. Not one of these churches has ever been the ceremonial headquarters of a bishop. But the nicknames show how Englishmen have come to regard a cathedral. It must, they feel, be the largest and most splendid church of some district. It must be a grand building, preferably cruciform, at least 300 feet long, and adorned by a central tower. It must be served by a Dean and Chapter, and its daily services must at least include a choral evensong. Its choir must be furnished with stalls, preferably adorned beneath their seats with an assortment of carved misericords. For some visitors it may, perhaps, be incidental that among the objects on which its clergy sit down a special seat is provided, and suitably adorned, for the bishop of its diocese.

Yet what makes a cathedral is not its size or its architectural beauty, but the presence within its choir or sanctuary of the *cathedra* ($K\alpha\theta\acute{\epsilon}\delta\rho\alpha$) or ceremonial seat from which the bishop presides, at various services, over gatherings of his clergy and of as many of the laity as can reach the building. In the days of the small, early, persecuted Church no cathedrals, as the Middle Ages understood them, could exist. For no Christian worship was allowed in public, and the overseers of the small Christian gatherings presided, where they could, in the houses of their faithful; the same conditions applied to England's Catholics in penal times and can still occur anywhere in times of persecution. Nor could cathedrals, as these buildings later grew, be built under the conditions of a small and struggling missionary body; an iron chapel or a glorified grass hut could still be the cathedral of a missionary

Bristol: sacristy vault, c. 1320

5 *A Cathedra,
Durham: Bishop
Hatfield's throne
and tomb, c. 1375*

bishop. Only when Christianity had become universal, and when the Church led a Godward-looking society, could one build the cathedrals which became the glory of mediaeval Europe. Under these conditions they were not merely the headquarters of a bishop whose diocese might not go beyond the area of a single town, but they had become the mother churches (though not always the largest churches) of areas larger than an English county. But in more difficult times a bishop's throne can be in a church which is no less a cathedral because it is much smaller than Amiens, Seville, Trondheim, St. John Lateran, or Lincoln. Many cathedrals in small Italian dioceses are of modest dimensions, while a bishop's throne, as in the Isle of Man since the ruination of St. German's cathedral, can be set, without loss of canonical status, in the bishop's private chapel.

But in mediaeval England cathedrals became large and splendid, lower in height than their French opposite numbers, but often of great length and with their upward-rising bulk enhanced by great central towers, and sometimes by spires, of which those at Lincoln, above Old St. Paul's in London, and at Salisbury were the tallest. Before the Reformation they were rivalled, and sometimes surpassed, by the churches of great abbeys. But the ruination of such monastery churches as Glastonbury, Reading, and Bury St. Edmund's has increased the cathedrals' dominance, while in a few cities the conversion into cathedrals of abbey churches left them secure, at Chester for example, as the chief churches of their shires.

Till the nineteenth century most English dioceses were of large though varying size. Mediaeval or Georgian bishops were often only occasionally resident. Nonetheless the cathedrals, particularly those like Salisbury which worked out their own liturgical 'uses', became important centres of worship and ceremony. The liturgical pioneers of western Christendom had long planned that cathedrals and great abbeys should perform their services with a splendour and good order which the parish churches of primitive Europe could not hope to attain. In such churches, particularly those of the Cluniac monks, High Mass could be celebrated with special splendour, and large communities of monks and canons could ensure, in the serried rows of their rectangular choir spaces, that their choir offices, from mattins to compline, were sung with a dignity only possible where large bodies of trained chanters were available. The choir space, which in most cathedrals contained the bishop's throne, and the sanctuary beyond it comprised the heart and centre of a great monastic or collegiate church. Here was what the Spaniards called the chief chapel—the *capilla mayor*—of the cathedral. Though lesser chapels existed, all else was subordinate to this relatively small area. The naves, particularly when lay worshippers deserted them for separate parish churches, were of much less note.

13

By 1150, and from then till the reign of Henry VIII, England's cathedrals numbered 19★. Those at Bath and Coventry lost their cathedral status when Henry VIII dissolved their monasteries and reduced their dioceses to one cathedral apiece. He also created six new bishoprics, making cathedrals of six dissolved monastic churches; one of these, Westminster Abbey, soon lost its new position.

Of the cathedrals which contained the thrones of mediaeval bishops some, as at Canterbury, York, Wells, and Worcester, had always been the chief churches of their dioceses. Some, as at Exeter, Norwich, and Chichester, had succeeded Saxon cathedrals elsewhere in their own counties, while at Salibury the comparatively new cathedral replaced one at Old Sarum which had itself succeeded Sherborne. Nine of the cathedrals, by an arrangement peculiar to England, were served by Benedictine monks. Carlisle had Augustinian canons regular. The rest had their Chapters composed of deans and canons, secular priests with no obligation of permanent residence. Their places (*vices*) in choir were thus often taken by *vicarii chorales* whose residential closes became a specially attractive feature of the precincts of these 'secular' cathedrals. Their staffing arrangements did not affect the plans of the cathedrals, each one of which needed a choir, a sanctuary for the high altar, floor space for the throne, aisles for circulating space and processions, and many side chapels. But the basis of their staffing *did* affect the layout, and the relationship to the church, of the domestic buildings. Where a cathedral was monastic one found the taut grouping round the cloister, and the immediate nearness to the church, of all monasteries. But the houses of deans, chancellors, precentors, and other secular canons were apt, as in the Barchesterian enclosures of Salisbury and Wells, to be widely spaced round the perimeter of closes, and sometimes in nearby streets. The bishop's Palace, one alone among a mediaeval prelate's houses in and out of his diocese, was a separate building, irrelevant to the plan of his cathedral church.

As mediaeval bishops often stayed away from their cathedral cities, and as many of them combined prelacy with the holding of high political posts, they varied in the interest they took in their cathedrals' fabric and adornment.

★Canterbury, York, Winchester, Durham, Rochester, London, Bath and Wells in the same diocese, Worcester, Hereford, Coventry and Lichfield for the same bishop, Ely, Norwich, Lincoln, Chichester, Exeter, Salisbury and Carlisle.

6   York: crossing and North transept, thirteenth cen

At Canterbury, and in some other monastic cathedrals, more was done by the priors of the cathedral monasteries than by the holders of the sees. But at Exeter several successive bishops keenly forwarded their cathedral's transformation. William of Wykeham's energy and architectural patronage caused the renewal of Winchester's nave. St. Hugh of Lincoln personally urged on building work on his cathedral, while at York the northern arch-bishops tended to do more for the fabric of the Minster than the Canterbury archbishops, mainly based on Lambeth, did for the cathedral where their tombs are more in evidence than their architectural endeavours.

Another thing which varied greatly was the money available for cathedral building. The bishops' incomes varied from the humble sums at Rochester and Carlisle to the princely revenues of the two archbishops and of the sees of Winchester and Durham. The cathedral priories, and the secular chapters, also varied greatly in their wealth. Pilgrimage shrines could help, though few if any attracted offerings on the scale of Becket's at Canterbury, But the modest scale of the cathedrals at Rochester and Carlisle, the low key of most work at Chichester, and at Hereford the moderate dimensions and generally Norman character of the pre-Reformation cathedral can all be explained by the lower finances available to those cathedrals than to the much larger cathedrals at Ely and Lincoln, or to the Chapters which commissioned the fine ornament at Exeter or Wells.

Though the cathedrals became important liturgical centres neither they nor the monastic churches were the ordinary worshipping places of the laity. Pilgrims would visit them as they also visited such monastic churches as Glastonbury and Walsingham, while those who made wills would often give legacies to 'mother churches' which they may never have seen. Important local families were often their benefactors, just as the descendants of those who had founded some abbey would make it gifts and find burial in its church; the Berkeley tombs in Bristol Cathedral (at first St. Augustine's Abbey) well remind us of such a connection. The chantry chapels and tombs of local magnates, and of the few kings buried in cathedrals, set up a tradition, richly continued, of cathedrals as the Valhallas of the county gentry.

The processes of building, and the artistic influences behind their gradual completion, were alike in the cathedrals, the abbeys, and great collegiate churches. All these buildings were professional jobs—designed by master masons and put up by men in the well-defined grades of the mediaeval building trade. The skilled masons, the setters and wallers, the rough layers, and the labourers all had their allotted tasks along with carpenters and joiners, the carvers of statues and niches, the glaziers, and the makers of such fittings and memorials as stalls, lecterns, and brasses. Bishops, deans, and priors naturally had an interest in what was done, but they were not the designers. What they could do, knowing the fabrics of other cathedrals and abbeys, was to borrow features of one church for use in another, and sometimes to ensure that a master mason who had done well on one great church was employed on another. It thus seems that when Prior Simeon of Winchester became abbot of Ely he employed on the latter church the designer responsible for the severe Norman transepts at Winchester. Durham Cathedral, thanks to the designers of its great Norman fabric, was widely influential elsewhere. The same master mason seems certain to have worked for the Norman abbots of Gloucester, Tewkesbury, and Pershore, while Bishop Roger of Old Sarum and his kinsman Alexander at Lincoln seem to have patronised the same designer alike for cathedrals and castles. Two centuries later a strong kinship of technique, though with different masons, was evident in the final creation of the eastern limbs at Lichfield and Wells, while the abbeys at Malmesbury and Glastonbury both borrowed the same 'stone cage' effect pioneered in the choir at Gloucester. William of Wykeham chose William of Wynford to finish the transformation of his great cathedral's nave, while in 1499 Bishop Oliver King, like Wykeham in having held high office at Court, chose Court architects, not local designers, to build his new cathedral at Bath.

Building work on cathedrals, great abbeys, and collegiate churches was usually slow. Though skilful and ingenious, mediaeval masons and builders lacked the technical resources for really quick construction, and the absence of a modern credit system meant that work had to be done as money came to hand. Shortages of money, and the financial strain of large-scale building, caused delays only partly overcome by benefactions from kings and other magnates. The modest new cathedral at Bath was begun in 1499, but was less than half complete when forty years later the dissolution of its monastery stopped work. The building of the new cathedral at Salisbury, from 1220 to its consecration in 1258, was supported as a national venture and was reckoned

17

as a quick job. But the original building did not include the central steeple, so that here, as at Worcester and Norwich and in a surviving structure at Chichester, the bells were hung in a separate tower. At Ely, and in the abbey church at Peterborough which Henry VIII made a cathedral, the naves were so slowly built that the last portions were in a different style from that used in the central and eastern parts of those Norman churches. But at Exeter the refashioning of the cathedral, during nearly a hundred years, was finished in the basic idiom used before 1300; the Black Death may partly have caused the delay. But such a building history meant that the nave's western end was architecturally outdated when it was complete. Some English mediaeval cathedrals were never quite completed, though none were so spectacularly unfinished as at Beauvais and Cologne. But at Ripon the late Gothic rebuilding of the crossing arches is clearly partial, while at Westminster Abbey the nave and its western towers had not been finished before the dissolution of 1540. No work was done during the church's few years as a cathedral, or when, under Mary I, it again became a monastic church. So the towers' completion had to await a scheme by Wren and its execution by Hawksmoor. In cathedrals and their attendant buildings, as in the domestic quarters and gatehouses of some monasteries, new work continued till the mid-Tudor decades of religious upheaval. The central tower at Wells got its fan vault in the 1520's, and in the same cathedral the simple Renaissance pulpit is some 20 years later. At Carlisle Lancelot Salkeld the last prior was the first dean when, about 1542, he put up a charming screen in the Renaissance taste. Classical motifs combine with late Gothic in the chantry, at Winchester, of Bishop Gardiner who erected it in the Catholic interlude under Mary I.

THE BUILDING PROCESS: ROMANESQUE

Little remains of the various cathedrals which housed the thrones of England's Anglo-Saxon bishops. Some have been obliterated by later buildings on their sites. Where Norman cathedrals were built on new sites foundation courses of the pre-Conquest buildings have only been revealed by excavation. Only at Sherborne, whence the bishops moved to Old Sarum, does a little of an Anglo-Saxon monastic cathedral remain above ground. A simple

7   *Canterbury contrasts: Norman, early Gothic and the Perpendicular 'Bell Harry' tower*

round-arched doorway survives at the western end of the present abbey. Experts think that some pre-Conquest masonry lies embedded in the piers of the nave, that this early cathedral was cruciform, and that its nave had aisles and a central and a western tower. Its style, like that of most late Saxon parish churches, must have been round-arched Romanesque, less ornamented than what the Normans eventually built, but belonging to the great architectural tradition which had, by about 1,000 A.D., spread all over western Europe. The windows, doorways and arches of England's other Saxon cathedrals probably displayed the same idiom.

The first cathedral at North Elmham in Norfolk was only a wooden chapel. But at Rochester a plain rectangular nave and round-apsed chancel had foundations, and presumably a superstructure, of stone. At Ripon St. Wilfred's early crypt is a rough and simple room, in its planning more akin to the *confessio*, or saint's burial chamber, of a Roman basilica than to the ambitious lower churches which lay beneath the eastern limbs of some Norman cathedrals. Simple basilican cathedrals, aisled and with great eastern apses, existed at York and Wells, while the later cathedral at Elmham had a long, narrow nave, with an eastern end whose transept and apse were given extra effect, as seen from the East, by two slim towers rising up, from the corners formed by the nave and transept walls, as staircase towers later rose above some Elizabethan mansions.

The most impressive Anglo-Saxon cathedrals were probably at Canterbury and Winchester. The archbishop's cathedral, when it was burnt in 1067, was an aisled basilica, some 200 feet long, with an apse at each end and a pair of flanking towers. At Winchester an early cathedral, with chapels on each side, became the eastern part of a far larger church, as at Canterbury over 200 feet long, and with an impressive pair of round-ended transepts which may have flanked a raised platform for the seating of royalty. The whole composition was Carolingian in its inspiration, an early version in England of the *west-werken* which ended the naves of some great post-Conquest churches.

The Anglo-Norman period saw the greatest changes which have come over England's cathedrals. Every cathedral, except perhaps that of Wells which temporarily lost its cathedral status and whose Gothic successor was started late in the twelfth century, was replaced where the headquarters of bishops were not moved, as from Wells to Bath and from Selsey to Chichester, to different towns. This wholesale building process was a revolutionary architectural act, determining that England's cathedral and large abbey churches should be of the size now considered 'cathedralesque'. The dimensions soon attained by the greater Benedictine and secular collegiate churches were also those duly achieved by the more notable Augustinian and Cistercian churches. Just as Saxon bishops and abbots made way for prelates of Continental birth and training so the ambitious scale of Norman planning and design, already seen in England and in Edward the Confessor's abbey at Westminster, entrenched itself, with even greater grandeur, in England's cathedrals and abbeys. Inside the large new churches the 'three tier' interior elevation of main arcades, triforium galleries, and rows of upper, or clerestory, windows, got firmly established. Some of these churches, as at Norwich, Peterborough, and Gloucester, remained, with minor elongations, till the sixteenth century. The Normans, unfairly as many now consider, despised the cultural and building work of the Anglo-Saxons. Abbot Paul of Caen, whose new church at St. Alban's was an early, dramatic example of the Norman architectural assault, but who did not disdain to re-use some Saxon balusters in the triforium of his own transepts, called the Anglo-Saxons *rudes et idiotas*. He was not, in such an opinion, alone among those who had 'come over with the Conqueror'. The pre-Conquest cathedrals and abbeys thus had small chances of survival. For another century the Romanesque tradition of round-arched building continued. It was, however, more grandly and more ornately expressed.

Liturgical needs determined the planning of the great Anglo-Norman cathedral and monastic churches. What monks and bodies of canons chiefly wanted was a choir cum sanctuary which could somewhere, though only in certain churches, contain a bishop's throne. Space was also needed for the ceremonies at the high altar, for processions and for dignified access from the sacristy to the side chapels required by the obligation, on those in priest's orders, to say a daily Mass. Hence the number of those chapels, at ground level, in the crypt, or even in the triforium. A sacristy and a Chapter House would be provided outside the main body of the church, but in the Anglo-Norman period there was still, in some monastic churches, the need to provide worshipping space for some of the laity dwelling in the town.

The choir, not yet made splendid by late Gothic canopied stalls, was placed

under the crossing tower or in the eastern sector of the structural nave. The space below the tower would, in such churches, be free for circulation. Beyond it the eastern limb, much shorter than the nave, would mostly consist of the sanctuary leading up to the high altar; only where a processional passageway, or ambulatory, ran behind the sanctuary was that altar far from the eastern wall. Chapels were fitted up at the eastern ends of choir aisles and off transepts. Where eastern limbs were not ended, as at Exeter, Lincoln, and most notably at St. Alban's, by a set of parallel apses, but on the 'periapsidal' plan surviving at Norwich and Gloucester they led off the ambulatories. Space for parishioners, screened off from the monks' or canons' portions and virtually separate churches, could be provided in the western parts of the naves, often built later than the eastern portions which were, for the monks and canons, of more practical and liturgical importance. The naves of England's Anglo-Norman cathedrals and abbeys were apt to be longer than their Norman opposite numbers. Some, as at Norwich and Winchester, were astonishingly long. One gets the impression of rivalry, and of long naves, like late Gothic towers, as something of status symbols. The western ends of these naves were often richly adorned with windows, wall arcading, and the sculpture of their doorways. These façades, whether or not they were widened out by the *westwerken* which came as a Germanic addition to the churches' mainly Norman character, were important in that they were, as the people of Rochester, Norwich, Ely, and Hereford saw them, a Norman cathedral's main chance of making a striking display to the town.

Few great Norman churches had central towers as high as those at St. Alban's, Tewkesbury, Southwell, and Norwich. More of them were squat and unimpressive, though at Winchester and Ripon their dignity was later increased by the addition of spires. At Old Sarum and Exeter the liturgical centre was graced not by a single crossing tower but, in the Rhenish manner, by one on each side of the choir. At their western ends, advancing on most examples in Normandy and setting a fashion which became the terminating glory of several English cathedrals, some Anglo-Norman cathedrals and abbeys had pairs of western towers. They appeared in Lanfranc's modest cathedral at Canterbury, at Southwell, and at Durham.

The monks' living quarters in the cathedral monasteries were at first less impressive than they became in the fourteenth century and in the period of

23

Like their thrones, the tombs of bishops are of the essence of cathedrals. Bishop Waynflete (d. 1486) lies at Winchester

the Perpendicular style. But fine Norman undercrofts, the basement storeys of buildings later renovated, survive at Durham and Chester. Some cloister walks were at first of wood, later replaced by the lovely vaulted and windowed alleyways which are major glories at Chester, Worcester, Norwich, Gloucester, and Canterbury. As the connecting walkways between buildings which had to be grouped close to the churches, cloister alleys were essential in any monastic cathedral. But in those served by secular canons they were something of a luxury, serving few buildings but the Chapter House and perhaps the library. Chapter Houses, for the business meetings of the monks and canons, were, however, an early requirement; from the great Anglo–Norman building wave they survive at Worcester, and best of all at Bristol.

The sheer size and massiveness of the Norman cathedrals was such that profuse decoration became subordinate to general effect. Columns, cylindrical or made up of a core and several shafts, sometimes had capitals adorned with scalloped decoration or with figure sculpture and foliate patterns on the capitals of smaller shafts, while some arches were edged with zig-zag moulding or other decoration. Though arches in sanctuaries, as at Norwich and Hereford, might get more decoration than in transepts, ornamental details were apt to be more pronounced in naves. These were often built later than eastern limbs, and in the twelfth-century decades when Norman builders and carvers produced their more ornate effects, and when, as at the West end of Ely Cathedral, pointed, 'Transitional Norman' arches had begun to appear. The western portals at Rochester and Lincoln are spectacular works of late Romanesque decoration, while at Ely the southern doorway (the Prior's door) is elaborate in the manner of contemporary illumination, or of the interior arches and outside doorways which, in small parish churches at Kilpeck and Barfreston, give an impression of overpowering decoration. In their original state, with small round-headed windows and in the absence of coloured glass, the Norman cathedrals must have gained opulence and colour from geometrical patterns painted on walls and arches, and from the designs on their painted ceilings.

By about 1100 the eastern limbs of many Anglo–Norman cathedrals were finished or nearly so. As their plans were based on the Latin cross their eastern sections were much shorter than their naves. Soon, however, there came the first stirrings of an urge to stretch out beyond the short confines of their apsidal presbyteries. At Old Sarum, the smallest of England's Norman cathedrals, and the one with the shortest eastern limb Bishop Roger, in possession of his see from 1107, soon drastically altered his hilltop cathedral. He gave it a longer, square-ended eastern limb, and a central tower to replace the Rhenish flanking towers of the earlier cathedral. The site did not permit really generous eastward elongation, but as Roger left it the cathedral was much longer, and by report much more splendid, than the building he had found; surviving masonry, beyond the North transept, which lay below the Treasury bears out reports on the high quality of the work. As Roger's new choir was being finished the new eastern limb arising at Canterbury was far larger, and more significant for the future of English cathedral planning, than the extensions at Old Sarum.

Archbishop Lanfranc's modest-sized cathedral, with its short eastern limb, was too small for its large Benedictine community, and fell far below the splendour felt right for an archbishop's church. Prior Ernulf and his successor Conrad took drastic steps to put things right. By an ambitious act of eastward elongation they built, beyond Lanfranc's crossing, a new eastern limb, nearly 200 feet long and so large, above its magnificent crypt or lower church, that it almost amounted to a complete new cathedral. To give extra altar space, it had the novelty of a pair of eastern transepts, while more chapels were sited in short towers which flanked its periapsidal East end. For the future planning of many cathedrals and abbeys the main thing about 'Conrad's Glorious Choir', which was finished in 1126, was that the monks who served Canterbury Cathedral when Becket was murdered there could all be seated, not in part of the nave or under the crossing tower, but more conveniently within the ample length of their new eastern limb.

GOTHIC ELONGATION

The renovation of the eastern limb at Canterbury was as much the result of an unforeseen accident as was the rebuilding, five centuries later, of St. Paul's in London. But at St. Paul's much Renaissance alteration, including the building of a central dome, had been planned by Wren before the fire of 1666; the new cathedral's style came logically from what Wren had proposed for parts of the mediaeval building. At Canterbury, in 1174, the gutting of the new choir was widely seen as an act of divine wrath for Becket's murder four years earlier. The early Gothic refashioning of the choir, above the undamaged crypt and within outer walls which were only half a century old and which the monks wished to keep, was not merely a memorial to St. Thomas and the preparation of a worthy setting for the martyr's shrine. The style of the new work, by a master mason whom Becket may personally have known, linked with the exile years of the archbishop's life.

True Gothic, or 'pointed' architecture, depending not merely on the shape of its arches but on the way in which the downward thrust of its ribbed vaults was concentrated, at intervals along the length of a nave or choir, where pillars and vaulting shafts marked the divisions between compartments or 'bays', had been evolved in the middle decades of the twelfth century. The new style first appeared in some abbeys and cathedrals near Paris. Pointed arches, stronger than those of the rounded shape, had been used in England since about 1150, being blended, as one sees in the western bays of the nave at Worcester, and in the *westwerk* at Ely, with rounded arches and decorative elements more typical of Norman Romanesque. But neither these, nor the contemporary 'Galilee', with richly adorned round arches, at the western end of the nave at Durham belonged structurally to mediaeval architecture's pointed phase. Nor, in the priory church which later became the cathedral at Oxford, was Gothic in evidence in the ingenious combination, under large round containing arches, of the main arcade and the triforium stage; only in the capitals, with their free-flowing foliage recalling Corinthian classical architecture, was there a break from the stiff conventions of Romanesque ornament. It was at Canterbury, in the transformed choir limb, that the real Gothic of northern France appeared in England.

The designer of the new choir at Canterbury was William of Sens, a master mason from the city in France where Becket had spent much of his exile. William had probably known Becket; he was also the designer of the new Gothic cathedral at Sens itself. The Canterbury monks' choice was thus most apt; what William gave them, and what William the Englishman supervised when the Frenchman went home after an accident, was a close adaptation, within the outer walls of the burnt eastern limb, of the choir at Sens. Here, for the first time in England, was true Gothic; it included, behind the High

9   Early English ensemble: the South choir arcade and Lady Chapel at Worces

Altar, an apsidal eastward extension giving ample space, before the circular Trinity Chapel which ended the cathedral, for the shrine of Becket after the saint's body had been brought up from the crypt. Despite some rounded arches and round-headed windows the impression in the simply vaulted choir and its eastern extension is wholly French Gothic; some details, particularly the paired columns whose design is echoed in the eastern part of the crypt, come straight from Sens.

Despite the impression it created the new choir at Canterbury had no immediate successors in England; like Henry III's new work at Westminster Abbey it remained a French Gothic exotic on English soil. English Gothic developed on its own, with squared East ends, internal heights much less than in most French cathedrals, and with an increasing fondness, as the Augustinians at Oxford soon showed in their steeple, for central towers and spires. Pointed arches and simply designed vaults became almost universal, and dogtooth ornament replaced Norman chevron patterns. Only in a few rounded arches, and in such details as the square-topped capitals of the earliest work at Wells, and in the choir arcades at Ripon, did Romanesque touches of design survive till about 1200. Hand in hand with the acceptance of the 'pointed' style went the continued urge for eastward elongation; the process was often enhanced by the building of eastern chapels for Masses and choir offices in honour of the Blessed Virgin Mary. Western additions such as the porch at Ely and the façade at Peterborough, and the vaulting of Norman presbyteries as at Hereford and Gloucester, or even the start, with the transepts, of vast rebuilding at York were less significant, for the all-important ground planning of cathedral or abbey churches, than these extensions of their eastern limbs.

At Chichester, where there was never much money to spare, the work done shortly before 1200 was not the elongation but the squaring off of an apsidal eastern end. Some details—rounded arches and foliate capitals in particular—were French in character and recalled the new work at Canterbury, but they gave no more than a northern French flavour to a basically English plan.

A retrochoir, in the 'Early English', or lancet, style was built at Winchester, with its roof at a lower level than that of the presbytery; beyond it lay the first part of a Lady Chapel whose eastern portion was built after 1500. At

Durham the eastern extension was the famous nine altars chapel, projecting as an eastern transept and giving the cathedral a T-shaped end. At Hereford and Norwich no more was achieved than the addition (at Hereford for the first time in England) of complete eastern Lady Chapels. But in Bristol, as later at Peterborough, abbey churches which duly became cathedrals had Lady Chapels built not as eastern elongations but, more conveniently for their sites, off northern transepts. These chapels had no direct links with the North aisles of their churches' eastern limbs. But at St. Frideswide's at Oxford an attractive early Gothic arcade linked the new Lady Chapel with the presbytery's northern aisle.

These changes were all in 'lancet' Gothic, seen in churches of high quality with clustered columns, foliate capitals, and simply patterned rib vaults. The same style appeared, larger and often with more ornament, in cathedrals and other great churches where eastward lengthening was on a grander scale. An important eastern addition, with a second pair of transepts and England's best surviving Gothic crypt, was made at Rochester. A choir limb with eastern transepts was put up at Worcester, while at Ely a splendid eastern limb arose beyond the Norman crossing. At Southwell the canons built a beautiful choir limb whose modest internal height dispensed with a triforium stage, while at Ripon an early Gothic choir limb had been started not long before 1200. At Carlisle a new choir arose about 1250, but in 1292 it was badly damaged by fire. More important still were some wholly new 'Early English' cathedrals.

At Southwark a serious fire early in the thirteenth century caused the almost total replacement of the Augustinian priory church which in 1905 became an Anglican cathedral. The new church was modest-sized and most attractive in a simple Early English style. At Wells, from about 1190, a new cathedral was started North of that which had, with some enlargement, survived from before the Norman Conquest. Though not at first given a long eastern limb it was nearly 50 years before the broad western façade, with many niches and statues but without the upper stages of its towers, was finished before the cathedral's consecration in 1239. Of far greater note was the building, on an empty, flood-prone site, of the new cathedral in the city of New Sarum. The bishop and his chapter desired, for reasons of convenience and because of quarrels with the castle garrison, to move from their

hilltop cathedral at Old Sarum to a site in the valley of the Salisbury Avon. Pope Honorius III gave permission for the transfer, and in 1220 Bishop Poore started work where no Saxon foundations or other remains could affect the new church's plan. The chance thus came to build a pattern-book English cathedral. It was given a long choir limb, a square-ended sanctuary, eastern transepts, and an eastern Lady Chapel. Devoid at first of a central tower and spire it contained all the elements needed in a large cathedral. Though most of its windows were in groups of lancets the earliest type of tracery (now called plate tracery) appeared in some transept windows, while the 'geometrical' designs of the later thirteenth century were foreshadowed in the unglazed openings of the triforium stage. Little altered once its main structure was finished Salisbury cathedral remained the Parthenon of England's early Gothic. The houses of its clergy, like its bishop's Palace, were somewhat distant, while the cloisters, commenced about 1263, only served the Chapter House. This, with its central pillar, branching vault, fine wall arcading, and large 'geometrical' windows, is a superb octagonal building, ranking high among the polygonal Chapter Houses fairly common in England and, like squared East ends and fan vaulting, distinctive of this country's Gothic.

The 'Geometrical' style, with large pointed windows subdivided by stone mullions and filled, in their upper portions, with somewhat rigid but increasingly complex tracery, was normal from about 1250 to 1300. The process of elongation continued, with some attention given to naves where Norman eastern limbs had already been replaced. At Lincoln a fine Early English nave, and a broad West front, had been built by 1250, while at St. Alban's the enormously long nave was ended in the same style. At Lichfield the new nave was started about 1250, in the late Geometrical idiom, with its western façade and spires finished when 'Geometrical' had yielded to the richer, more flowing adornment of 'Decorated'. This nave was still designed on the 'three-tier' pattern of arcade, triforium, and clerestorey. But as it was none too high inside there was no room, above its large triforium arches, for clerestorey windows of the normal shape. So the builders put up the set of triangular but convex-sided windows, with geometrical patterns in their tracery, which gave Lichfield some distinctive designs.

But the eastward extension of choir limbs, and the provision of more side chapels, was still thought more pressing than the renewal of naves. At Lincoln

31

Romanesque and varyingly dated Gothic blend in the West front at Lincoln

the 'Angel' Choir was added to the existing choir built by St. Hugh; its main purpose was to allow space for the shrine of the lately canonised bishop. At Ripon the refashioning of the choir limb produced a spectacular Geometrical East window. In London, the policy of elongation was dragged out *ad absurdum* in the new eastern limb, above a splendid Gothic crypt or lower church, at Old St. Paul's. For the new work, with no second transepts to break its eastward run, had no less than 12 bays; Hollar's seventeenth-century engraving suggests that the screen and altarpiece failed to mitigate the impression of a long, low, vaulted tunnel which could logically have continued for another hundred feet.

Soon before 1300 the stiffness of geometrical tracery began to yield to more flowing and graceful 'Decorated' patterns. At Exeter the eastern Lady Chapel was built about this time, foreshadowing the coming style and a first item in the cathedral's complete rebuilding, between its Norman flanking towers and within its older aisle walls. The Lady Chapel had first been a separate building, and the scheme included the filling of the gap between the chapel and the Norman eastern wall. The result of some decades of activity was an eastern limb much longer than the Norman presbytery arm. At Wells and Lichfield a very similar policy was followed. In each cathedral the first eastern building was a separate Lady Chapel shaped as an elongated octagon. In both of them the master masons of the fourteenth century lengthened out an older eastern limb to create a single building. Earlier Gothic choir arcades were left standing, but the construction, above that level, of new upper stages and vaults created a unified impression all the way from the central tower to the sanctuary; at Wells (the richer of the two cathedrals) the work was of special delicacy and splendour. Important work seems also to have been done on the three-spired cathedral at Coventry. But as little of it survives bar excavated portions its elevations and details remain unknown.

More pioneering was the design of the new eastern limb of the Augustinian abbey church at Bristol. A new choir, with an eastern Lady Chapel to replace one, of about 1230, which ran out from the North transept, superseded the Norman presbytery. What makes this work unique among the choir limbs of England's cathedrals is the treatment of the one example of such a choir which has no clerestorey and whose aisles, as in a German 'hall church', are as high as the central alleyway. What the Bristol canons and their unknown

33

Lincoln: the Chapter House, thirteenth century

master mason planned was to combine the aisleless, 'college chapel' effect of the splendid new chapel of St. Stephen at Westminster with the aisles needed to give access to the chapels required in a monastic church. Internal flying buttresses, cross arches, and transverse tunnel vaults spanned the aisles to transmit the central vault's thrust to sturdy outer buttresses. The resulting impression, maybe deliberate but perhaps incidental to the architectural solution of a double problem, was a new one of sideways space. Allied with other rarities of vault and tomb design, and with some fine sculptural detail, this work of the early fourteenth century makes Bristol cathedral a prime pilgrimage place for architectural connoisseurs.

At Ely the unique work of the fourteenth century was prompted not by the desire for a longer eastern limb but by the damaging fall of the Norman central tower. The unusually wide, square-ended Lady Chapel was the century's addition to the cathedral's ground plan. The square crossing space was widened out into a spacious octagon; above it a timber lantern tower was poised above four great arches, four splendid Decorated windows, and a set of upward-curving timber vaulting ribs. More conventional, but almost rococo in its riot of ornament, was the three-tiered rebuilding of that part of the Early English choir which the falling tower had wrecked. At York, in the meantime, a future style had been foreshadowed in the bay design of the lofty new nave. Though the triforium gallery, of small practical use, had now been cut out in the eastern parts of such churches as Pershore Abbey and Southwell Minster it was kept at York. But the mullion lines of the upper windows continued downwards as the division between the triforium arches, uniting the nave's two upper stages into a single unit whose emphasis was less horizontal than vertical.

UPWARD SURGE

From about 1330, and for the next 200 years, not much was added to the ground areas of England's great abbeys and cathedrals. New Lady Chapels like those at Ely and Gloucester, the squaring off of the East end at Peterborough, some projecting chantry chapels at Salisbury, Hereford, and Canterbury, and new polygonal Chapter Houses at Hereford and Old St.

Paul's, accounted for most of the two-dimensional extension. More remarkable was the vertical emphasis of England's final Gothic style, the raising of the ceilings in such eastern limbs as those of Norwich and Gloucester, and along the much transformed nave at Winchester, and the impact on the city skylines of the great central towers which became a special architectural glory of England.

The cathedrals and great abbeys, and such collegiate churches as those at Beverley and Windsor, also became richer and more varied in the coloured splendour of their contents. After about 1280 they received most of what now survives by way of such details as canopied choir stalls, carved stall ends, misericords, lecterns*, altarpieces, sedilia and painted glass. Effigies had indeed started, and were made in increasingly high relief, from well before 1200. Some, like that of King John at Worcester, were later given higher tomb chests, while their sheer numbers, on altar tombs or in canopied recesses of varied elaboration, grew greatly by the middle decades of the sixteenth century. Some brasses, particularly for clerics below a bishop's or an abbot's rank, were also laid down, and the sadly empty matrices in floor slabs at Ely and Lincoln prove that those cathedrals once had them in dozens. But nowadays our cathedrals are poor in brasses, and except at St. Alban's and Hereford they are not a rubber's happy hunting ground. But their wealth of delicately

*Three of the finest brass lecterns, at Canterbury, Lincoln and Wells, are of the Restoration period, being by the London brassfounder William Burroughes.

12   Wells: a misericord, fourteenth century

beautiful chantry chapels, screened off in side chapels or on island sites in cagelike enclosures, all came late in the Middle Ages, particularly at Wells and Salisbury, and at Winchester where Bishop Gardiner's chantry, renewing the practice of chantry foundations under Mary I whom the bishop had married in that cathedral, is late enough to mix Renaissance detail with a basically Gothic design.

All this was done at a time for which our knowledge, from such documents as contracts and fabric rolls, becomes wider and more certain. The names of those who designed the Romanesque abbeys and cathedrals are virtually lost. From the thirteenth century, and still more from the late Gothic period, we know the names, and some details of the lives, of many master masons, and some craftsmen, who created and altered England's great churches as they existed when the Reformation brought great religious changes, and not a little physical destruction.

The 'Perpendicular' style, with its vertically panelled effects, with its emphasis, in window tracery, on upright lines to replace curvilinear patterns, and with shallow-headed arches over windows and in arcades, did not emerge, complete and new, in the transformation and reroofing of the choir and presbytery at Gloucester. The nave at York, St. Stephen's Chapel at Westminster, the new Chapter House at Old St. Paul's, the transomed choir windows at Bristol and the work at Gloucester all played their part in the evolution of England's distinctive late Gothic style. But the new choir at Gloucester, with its eastern wall nearly all one vast window, saw the coming fashion's fullest early statement. Fan vaults, with rich panelling on the under sides of masonry cones, were not at first thought safe over the main expanses of choirs and naves. The earliest examples, over the Chapter House at Hereford and the new cloister walks at Gloucester, and other specimens over such features as tower spaces, porches, and chantries, covered restricted areas; only towards the end of the Perpendicular period did Sherborne Abbey, the new cathedral at Bath, and King's College chapel at Cambridge see fan vaults on a monumental scale.

The developed Perpendicular style was seen, with lofty arches, transomed windows, and richly ribbed lierne vaults, in Henry Yevele's new nave at Canterbury, and at Winchester where Bishop William of Wykeham employed William of Wynford to transform and heighten the great Norman nave. The choir limb at York, a late phase in a great scheme of rebuilding started about 1240, retained some Decorated elements along with a generally Perpendicular idiom. Much later, in the years each side of 1500, the naves at Chester and Ripon, (neither of them yet cathedral churches) were rebuilt in differing versions of Perpendicular, while the one almost wholly new Perpendicular cathedral was started at Bath, about 1499, much smaller than its Norman Romanesque predecessor yet never finished before its monastery was dissolved and it lost its cathedral status. Its designers, the Court architects Robert and William Vertue, were in the main confined within the length of the earlier nave, re-using older foundations so that the central tower, with an East to West length only that of an ordinary nave bay, is rectangular in plan.

In some other cathedrals Perpendicular changes touched important details rather than main fabrics. At Norwich the splendid vaulting of the nave, transepts, and presbytery showed that complex lierne vaults, with a multitude of carved bosses, were a valid feature till about 1500, while at Wells the central crossing was fan vaulted as late as the 1520's. At Oxford the priory church of St. Frideswide got a choir vault, of great charm, in which details normal in fan vaulting were introduced into a rich vault in the main of the lierne type. The work was finished after 1500; similar treatment was started in the transepts, but was held over when Wolsey had the priory dissolved to provide the site, and the financial nucleus, of Cardinal College. More common than new vaulting was the alteration of windows, or drastic refenestration, made easy by the great amounts of glass that were now available, thus gratifying the urge to flood dark churches with more natural light. Norman windows at Durham and Gloucester, and early Gothic lancets at Wells, were filled with Perpendicular tracery, while at Southwell, Rochester, Norwich, and Hereford the numerous windows of Romanesque West fronts made way for great single windows with their many lights, transoms, and the vertically planned tracery compartments of the Perpendicular style.

The upward thrust of late English Gothic had been displayed, before the full acceptance of 'Perpendicular', in some splendid central towers; their effect was sometimes enhanced, as at Lincoln, Hereford, and London, or by surviving structures at Lichfield and Salisbury, by spires. In such towers horizontal subdivisions could be masked, as one notes at Wells, and at Lincoln where the central tower of soon after 1300 is the highest of all, by the strong

upward emphasis of tall, narrow windows and panelled walls. Even at Hereford, where the tower is of modest height and where the two stages are horizontally parted, the panels and windows are slender enough to convey an upward feeling.

The same vertical emphasis appeared in the fully Perpendicular central towers. The first and one of the finest, complete by 1375, was at Worcester. Those at York and Durham, like the two somewhat earlier western towers at Wells, are unpinnacled; the corner pinnacles planned at York were left out to lessen the weight on the crossing piers. But at Gloucester the great central tower, of the middle decades of the fifteenth century, has battlements and tall corner pinnacles, traceried like shrines, which make the whole composition a pierced and pinnacled crown which influenced the design of parish church towers at Cardiff, in Bristol, and elsewhere in the western counties. At Bristol the central tower of what duly became the cathedral is short and stocky by the standard of Gloucester. But its tall, narrow panels and window openings still give an impression of an elevation greater than the tower's actual height.

The last and greatest of England's Perpendicular central towers was at Canterbury Cathedral; it was supported not only by the crossing piers but by a beautiful set of early Tudor strainer arches across three of the tower arches and the eastern end of each nave aisle. The tower, with eight pinnacles and strong vertical lines at its corners and up its sides, was finished to John Wastell's designs and had a gilded angel to crown one of its pinnacles. It was finished in the 1490's; from then onwards (Bath apart) little was added to the main fabrics of the English cathedrals.

Yet work continued, till the end of the pre-Reformation period, on attendant buildings. Cloister walks and the domestic buildings of cathedral monasteries were often altered, or rebuilt, in the Perpendicular style. At Wells the Deanery was almost wholly renewed in the last quarter of the fifteenth century, while some vicars' closes, particularly at Hereford and Wells, are mostly of this period; the 'Barchester' image was largely a late Gothic creation. The approach to cathedral or monastic precincts by dignified gateways had started some centuries before. But several of these gate towers came in the heyday of the Perpendicular style. Those at Norwich and Wells, and at Salisbury as one approaches the Close from the city, are particularly well known. At Canterbury the splendidly ornamented Christ Church gate-

Mainly Early English: the stupendous western façade at Peterborough

way, richly panelled and with the arms and badges of the king who later had Becket's shrine despoiled and the cathedral monastery dissolved, was finished about 1517. The new gateway to the Augustinian precincts at Carlisle came in 1527, less than ten years before the start of the political and religious upheaval which changed the régime, and soon increased the number, of the English cathedrals.

POST-REFORMATION

By the end of 1540 the cathedral monasteries had been dissolved, while Bath and Coventry were no longer cathedral cities. But for the next few years the cathedrals of England saw little physical or architectural change. The demolition of the nave at Bristol was the most important act of truncation. Retrochoirs lost their purpose once the shrines of their saints had been dismantled, and altars disappeared from chantry chapels once the institution of chantries had been abolished. Deans and secular Chapters replaced the monks of the monastic cathedrals and of the abbey churches promoted to cathedral rank. More drastic changes came under Edward VI. Many sanctuary fittings and other furnishings were destroyed, side chapels were robbed of their altars, while roods and other images suffered severely. But then and under Elizabeth I the Anglican Church retained bishops. The cathedrals thus kept their thrones and their status. The numerous pre-Reformation choir offices made way for Prayer Book mattins and evensong, sung in choirs still solidly screened from the naves of their cathedrals. The naves still served little liturgical purpose; comparative disuse yielded, in some of them and notoriously at Old St. Paul's, to outright profanation.

Routine maintenance was still carried out, but the cathedrals saw few structural changes in the hundred years from Henry VIII's time to the start of the Civil War. Diminution and impoverishment were more normal, some of it deliberate, but by accident when in 1561 the great timber spire of Old St. Paul's was burnt away. It was on this cathedral that the only architectural work of real importance occurred before the Civil War. For the dilapidated Norman nave and transepts were much altered and given a partially classical aspect. Inigo Jones carefully transformed and embellished the end walls of the transepts and the entire outside of the nave. Pilasters masked the shallow Norman buttresses and round-headed windows, below circular openings, echoed Romanesque window forms. Western towers, with cupolas, foreshadowed Wren's later design. Across the West front a great Corinthian colonnade, balustraded and crowned by statues, was among the finest pieces of classical architecture then put up in England.

The Civil War and the years of the Commonwealth brought interior devastation, and some structural damage, to most English cathedrals. Much coloured glass was destroyed, and there was heavy destruction of mediaeval and Laudian fittings. The Restoration ushered in a period of repair and refitting which lasted into the eighteenth century. The cathedrals' main fabrics were less affected than the arrangement of their choirs. At Lichfield the central steeple, and some window tracery, were renewed much as they had been before the siege of 1643. But at Carlisle no effort was made to rebuild the demolished main portion of the nave. The most ambitious work was that planned, but never started, at Old St. Paul's. Wren got out designs whereby the nave's interior would have been classicised, with giant Corinthian pilasters as its chief new feature. Wren also planned to open out the central crossing into an octagonal space in the manner of the octagon of his uncle's cathedral at Ely. The piers were to support a slender, unattractive dome capped not by a lantern but by a thin, unhorticultural pineapple. Wren presented his plans only a few days before the great fire which in the end compelled a wholly new building. One should, however, note that the conception of a domed St. Paul's goes back before the historic blaze.

For the rest of the seventeenth century, and in the Georgian period till the earliest restoration schemes, not much was done to the cathedrals' main fabrics. At Ely some attractive work in the Wren manner was done, mostly by Robert Grumbold of Cambridge and on the North transept. At Lincoln Gibbs designed strengthening walls, and some round-headed arches, beneath the western towers, while at Hereford two massive early Georgian piers, with half arches above them, sustained the weight of the central tower. The one great Renaissance work, on a cathedral whose wholly new fabric made it unique in England, was Wren's St. Paul's. The idea of its dome was no novelty. But so complete a church in Franco-Italian Baroque was wholly unlike what Englishmen had come to accept in cathedrals. Yet in its plan, with an eastern

41

limb nearly as long as its nave, the new St. Paul's was an English mediaeval cathedral in Renaissance dress. From a distance, as it rises above the older rooftops of the City, its dome belies its great difference, in plan, from St. Peter's in Rome or the congregational churches, with short sanctuaries and easily seen High Altars, which the Jesuits and their followers had pioneered. St. Paul's, moreover, like England's mediaeval cathedrals both before and after their Restoration refurnishing, had its choir parted by the screen, and the organ upon it, from its central space and its nave.

Except at Durham, where Bishop Cosin's Laudian conservatism gave a mainly Gothic flavour to the new font canopy and choir stalls, the post-Restoration refurnishing of cathedral choirs was almost wholly in the re-strained Baroque of the Wren school. Classical stalls and altarpieces, lecterns and brass chandeliers combined with the rich plush of stall and pulpit cushions, and with black and white marble paving, to give a sense of placid dignity, and of the 'solemn neatness' which, about 1712, a Bristol rhymer found in the cathedral and the refurbished churches of that opulent city.

No cathedral choir now remains as it was in these days of a restored, increasingly complacent Anglicanism; prints, engravings, and watercolours must be our evidence for their Georgian appearance. But this period's artistic achievement, detested by the Victorians and almost wholly swept away, was far from contemptible. From organ cases, from stalls at Durham and Canterbury, from glass like that of the 1660's surviving at Bristol, from Baroque gems like the font at Exeter, and even more from the noble monuments which were lavishly erected, one can realise that the enclosed choirs and draughty naves of England's cathedrals still vaunted some splendour.

Kent's screen at Gloucester, and the fine Chippendale Gothic pulpit at Lincoln came as touches of romantic Gothicism in cathedral furnishings. But the plaster vault which once covered the choir at Carlisle, and James Essex's important building and furnishing work at Lincoln, belong to the early phase of the comparatively correct Gothic Revival. So too did James Wyatt's much needed repair jobs on four cathedrals. Deeply as one must regret his demolition of two Perpendicular side chapels and the detached belfry at Salisbury, and of most of Durham's Norman Chapter House, Wyatt deserves more credit than he has had for his wooden nave vault at Hereford, and for the new western end of the nave with which he replaced the Norman

43

French and Italian Baroque forms combine in Wren's final version of the western façade at St. Paul's

West front destroyed, in 1786, by the collapse of the tower which fourteenth-century builders had unwisely placed on slender supports. In one respect, moreover, Wyatt's restorations and rearrangements took account of the historic past—unlike some Victorian Deans and architects, he made no effort to create single churches of normally subdivided cathedrals, but left choirs screened off from naves which ran too far West to be convenient as unified worshipping spaces.

Other architects, like L. N. Cottingham on a new, spireless central tower at Rochester, and George Austin with his Perpendicular north-western tower at Canterbury, continued, in the last few pre-Victorian years, the work of restoration and rebuilding.

VICTORIAN AND EDWARDIAN

The Victorian age was one of vast activity on the cathedrals' fabrics, on their scheme of worship, and for the greater number of people who could, thanks to modern transport, visit and admire them. Restoration, though sometimes too drastic, and crudely disrespectful of windows in the Perpendicular style, often saved buildings from outright ruin after long spells of decay and neglect. The tower and spire at Chichester did, indeed, collapse in 1861; the present steeple is a good reconstruction by that prolific renovator Sir George Gilbert Scott. Drastic refurbishing, in Victorian Gothic to replace despised Restoration classicism, was much in evidence, with pierced metal screens, as at Salisbury, Lichfield and Hereford, opening out new vistas from long naves to distant sanctuaries. Refurnishing and reglazing varied much from cathedral to cathedral; the process was notably drastic at Salisbury, Lichfield, Worcester, and in the choir at Canterbury.

Among structural changes the most important was the new nave at Bristol, designed by Street on the model of the unique choir limb and built, from 1867, in hopeful anticipation of the Bristol bishopric's restoration.* At Southwark too, by 1897, a new nave was built, with a similar hope that the one-time Augustinian priory church might soon be a cathedral. Sir Arthur Blomfield based his three-tiered, conventionally Early English design on the existing

*It had, in 1836, been amalgamated with that of Gloucester.

44

choir. Less innovating, but greatly changing the aspect of some cathedrals, were new eastern walls and windows, harking back to presumed original designs, at Oxford and Worcester, while at St. Alban's restoration work started by Scott was ruthlessly and controversially finished by Lord Grimthorpe who radically altered the transept ends, and built a new western façade blending Early English and Geometrical. The urge for new West fronts continued, soon after 1900, when Oldrid Scott designed a somewhat fussy, over-detailed façade to replace Wyatt's simpler work at Hereford.

Two new cathedrals were those at Truro and Liverpool. Pearson's building at Truro was started in 1880, of the modest size of Rochester, Bristol, or Ripon but a successful blend of Early English and French Gothic of the thirteenth century. The genuinely late mediaeval South aisle of St. Mary's parish church was cleverly preserved as an outer South aisle of the choir. At Manchester R. H. Carpenter's design for a vast cathedral, early Decorated with a central octagon like that at Ely, was never attempted, while at Liverpool no start was made on the initial project for a large Gothic cathedral close below St. George's Hall. Giles Gilbert Scott's scheme for the great cathedral on the St. James' Mount site was accepted in 1902–3, and its (liturgically) south-eastern Lady Chapel was started in 1904. As with Wren's 'Warrant' design for St. Paul's Scott made drastic changes in his designs for the main building; no one could have foreseen, when the young architect got his award for a somewhat conventionally Gothic design, with a pair of flanking towers, that what Liverpool would actually get was the single-towered 'Arts and Crafts' Gothic masterpiece whose completion has yet to be achieved.

OTHER CATHEDRALS

Between 1836 and 1927 the Church of England created 20 new bishoprics, mostly in areas where population changes demanded pastoral redeployment. Four of the new bishops, and the holder of the revived see of Bristol, had their thrones in churches of the conventionally cathedralesque type. Truro and Liverpool built cathedrals on traditional lines. The same happened, more recently and possibly for the last time in England, at Guildford. Here, as at Liverpool, a cathedral on a new site replaced a Georgian church which had

45

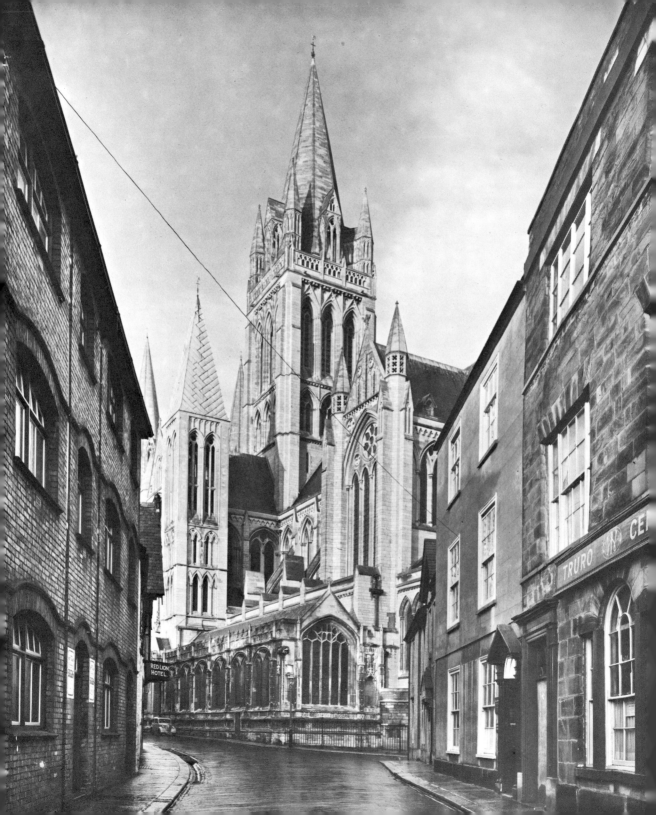

16 Liverpool: Anglican cathedral, the liturgical East end

served as a 'pro-cathedral'. Started in 1936, Sir Edward Maufe's Gothic building is cruciform, with transepts, a central tower, a choir limb, a nave, and some carefully planned attendant buildings; it also serves as the parish church of an upland suburb near the new University.

The remaining modern bishoprics had their thrones placed in parish churches—as a rule in the oldest and most historic church in each newly honoured cathedral city. Hence the cathedral status of what started as parish churches in Wakefield and Chelmsford, of Archer's Baroque St. Philip's in Birmingham and of All Saints' at Derby, by Gibbs and architecturally akin

Truro: mediaeval work blends with Victorian Gothic

(bar its noble late mediaeval tower) to St. Martin's in the Fields. At Blackburn the church of the 1820's is the most recent of these 'parish church' cathedrals. St. Michael's at Coventry, spacious and with many chapels and the surviving rarity of a Perpendicular apse, was the cathedral bombed in 1940 and now replaced, across the site of the city's older monastic cathedral, by the modern one designed by Sir Basil Spence.

The architecture and fittings of the 'parish church' cathedrals are not equal to those which the more traditional cathedrals can display. Yet these later cathedrals are not without excellent features, worth seeing if one happens to visit the cities concerned. Collegiate before the Reformation, the dignified, five-aisled building at Manchester has early sixteenth-century stalls, of the Ripon school, as good as the best elsewhere. At Newcastle the flying struts, in the Scottish manner upholding a central pinnacle, give the mediaeval tower an ancient upper feature unique in England. The thirteenth-century double bays of the cathedral at Portsmouth are an admirable rarity. At Birmingham and Derby the Renaissance quality of the architecture makes both buildings unusual among their fellows. The mere fact that all these churches have as their principal item of furnishing the ceremonial seat of an Anglican bishop makes them as much cathedrals as those whose fabrics are more stately, and whose staffing includes Deans and canons, along with the non-parochial status, of the cathedrals which had that rank till the beginning of the Victorian age. Yet in some of those cities people have been moved by the deep-rooted English feeling that a cathedral must be long and cruciform, with a choir more elaborate than that which can be contrived in the average parish church chancel. Hence the extensions and elongations, at Bradford, Blackburn, Bury St. Edmund's, Sheffield and elsewhere, which have brought these buildings into closer harmony with England's notion of the cathedral-esque.

Similar ideas have also been at work in some cathedrals of another group, now numbering 17 in England, which has only existed since 1850. A Roman Catholic hierarchy, with territorial dioceses having fixed headquarters, was then set up to replace the bishops who had, as Vicars Apostolic and without cathedrals, functioned since the reign of James II. Suitable buildings, most of them already parish churches and only three built with cathedral status from the start, contained the thrones of the new bishops and became their cathedrals.* All but two of the first group of England's modern Roman Catholic cathedrals were wholly Victorian, though some, like St. Chad's in Birmingham, replaced earlier churches on the same sites. Two of the bishop's thrones of 1850, including that of Cardinal Wiseman of Westminster, were housed in 'Pro' cathedrals. As in some new Anglican dioceses the feeling arose that some of England's Catholic bishops should be based in more stately buildings. Hence the projects for two Merseyside cathedrals by E. W. Pugin, one at Birkenhead for the Shrewsbury diocese, the other (actually started) at Everton for the bishop of Liverpool. Three separate designs were

*For more on the Roman Catholic cathedrals of England and Wales, see Bryan Little, *Catholic Churches Since 1623*, publ. 1966.

17 Coventry: the High Altar and Graham Sutherland's tapestry

D

made for a great Gothic cathedral in Westminster. Cardinal Vaughan, with Bentley as his architect, then built the large basilica, Byzantine in its inspiration, which was the English Catholics' one cathedral on the scale traditional in this country, and mediaevally cathedralesque in its staffing and liturgical routine. But most of England's Roman Catholics, a minority denomination and with much poverty in their ranks, had to stay content with the modest cathedrals fitted out in 1850 or built within the next 60 years. 'Cathedralesque' planning, with transepts and in the first case with an eastern Lady Chapel, was indeed seen, on a modest scale, at Nottingham, Plymouth, and Salford. E. W. Pugin's cathedral at Northampton, not lengthened eastwards till the 1950's, would have been cathedralesque in feeling, though not cruciform, while the impression of a small French Gothic cathedral was achieved, with the Duke of Norfolk's benefactions, in the great church at Arundel which had to wait till 1965 for a bishop's throne.

The oldest, and what could have been the most interesting of these parish church cathedrals was never finished as its sponsors hoped. The church of the Apostles was started, in Clifton, in 1834. Its architect, H. E. Goodridge of Bath, was both a Gothic and a classical designer. But Bishop Baines, Vicar Apostolic of the Western District and the chief ecclesiastic behind the scheme, was a passionate classical enthusiast. The ambitious, porticoed Corinthian church would, had it been quickly completed to Goodridge's designs, have been England's largest, most imposing Catholic church. But difficulties both with money and the subsoil caused the project to be held up till in 1848 Charles Hansom ingeniously fitted up the unfinished shell as a church which in 1850 became Clifton diocese's 'Pro' cathedral. The church is now being replaced, but on another site.

In the meantime, at Liverpool, the long story of unfulfilled schemes ended in 1967 with the opening of Sir Frederick Gibberd's great concrete-strutted pavilion with its splendidly glazed lantern tower. Sir Edwin Lutyens' project for a vast, domed neo-Renaissance cathedral had been started; its splendid crypt is below, and adjoining, the site of the new building. The cathedral's main structure is circular; chapels of varying size and shape surround the main space whose sanctuary is in the middle and whose throne has been hard to locate in any really focal spot. The designers took account of ideas accepted in the first phase of the modern liturgical revolution. Seating in a unified

Westminster Cathedral: saucer domes and campanile

worshipping space is so arranged that no one can be more than 70 feet from the High Altar. The building is both a parish church and a cathedral, but so large an auditorium comes more into its own on special and diocesan occasions than for the Sunday by Sunday worship of its parishioners and chance visitors.

Division between regular and special uses should hardly apply in the new Catholic cathedral at Clifton. Its planning, completed after the liturgical decisions of the Second Vatican Council, should make it among the World's

19   *Liverpool: Catholic cathedral, pavilion, porch and lantern*

most up-to-date cathedrals; its throne, behind the High Altar and backed by a low concrete wall, will be a better focus of attention than the *cathedra* at Liverpool. Sir Percy Thomas and Son are the architects of the concrete-built church, with its lantern supporting a 'flêche' whose two main arms will contain a cross; completion is due early in 1973. Though spacious, and allowing for episcopal ceremonies in a sanctuary larger than that at Liverpool, the main worshipping space will be more attuned than that cathedral's great three-quarter circle to the regular needs of a large parish than to the numbers expected on exceptional occasions. This carefully thought out building will depart, more than most other modern cathedrals, from the traditional notion of a building which developed, as two worshipping spaces under one roof, and which is primarily a splendid setting for the liturgical activities of a bishop and his Chapter. In an age when Christianity works in a social setting more akin to minority or persecution times than to those of the theocentric Middle Ages it will thus come closer to the notion whereby a bishop's church is also the normal worshipping place of a good proportion of his flock.

Bristol

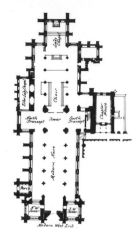

The cathedral at Bristol, of modest size but most important for students of rare and beautiful architecture, is one of six abbey churches which gained cathedral status under Henry VIII. The original diocese included Bristol, a little of southern Gloucestershire, and Dorset. In 1836 it was merged with that of Gloucester and the see was revived, with different boundaries, in 1897.

From the 1140's the church had been that of the Augustinian canons regular of St. Augustine's Abbey. Its nave had decayed and was pulled down, leaving a truncated church as England's smallest cathedral. The present nave and western towers, by G. E. Street and clearly indebted to the choir limb and to French Gothic, are Victorian; they were built, in the hope that the diocese would be revived, during the Gloucester amalgamation.

The chief surviving part of the Norman church is the South transept which is approached, from the level of the canons' dormitory, by the well preserved night stairway. More impressive, with its arched and vaulted vestibule and probably of about 1155, is the splendidly arcaded and enriched Chapter House—the finest Norman Chapter House in the country. The first, or 'elder' Lady Chapel off the North transept is exquisitely detailed 'Early English' work of about 1230.

Bristol Cathedral's uniquely important contribution to English architecture lies in the basic design, and in some of the details, of its early fourteenth-

54

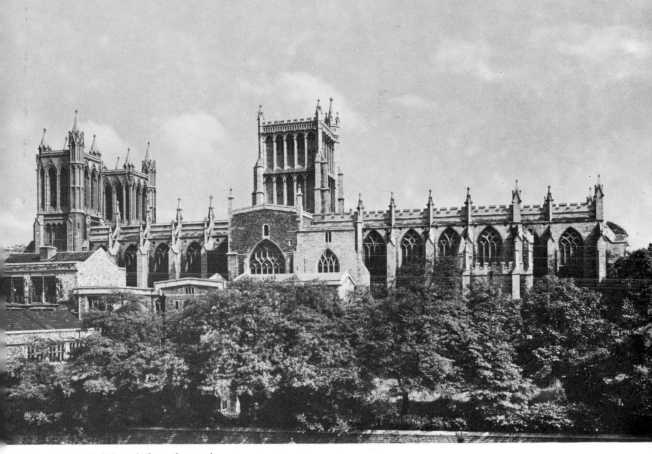

century eastern limb. The triforium and clerestorey were omitted, and the aisles are as high inside as the central alleyway. The external effect of an unaisled 'collegiate' chapel, like that of St. Stephen's, Westminster was thus harmonised with the demands of a community needing aisles to lead to several small eastern chapels and a new Lady Chapel; an incidental result was an innovating feeling of sideways space. The thrust of the central vault was upheld by a unique set of internal flying buttresses and cross arches. The 'flying' ribs of the sacristy vault are another rarity, and the outer decoration of the unusual 'stellar' tomb recesses anticipates, and may have inspired, similar work, of about 1500, in churches in Spain and Portugal.

The central tower and the transept vaults are of the fourteenth century, and the uniquely good set of abbots' effigies is of the same period. The cathedral is rich in other monuments—mediaeval, Renaissance, and Georgian, while fine fourteenth-century glass is accompanied by the rarity of some good glass of the 1660's. The fine silver candlesticks of 1712 were given by one of the sponsors of Woodes Rogers' great privateering voyage which included the rescue of Alexander Selkirk—the main original of Crusoe.

21   *The Norman Chapter House, c. 1155*

22 *The choir,*
central alleyway

Canterbury

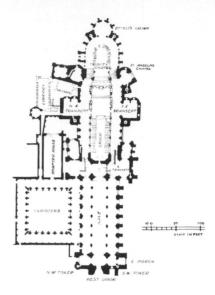

The diocese of Canterbury is the senior of those set up in England after St. Augustine's rechristianising mission landed in Kent in 597. As the cathedral of the southern archbishop and primate of England, as the scene of Becket's murder in 1170, and as the most famous and most frequented of England's mediaeval pilgrimage shrines Canterbury is the most historic, and perhaps the greatest of England's mediaeval cathedrals. Whatever other cathedrals one knows, a visit to Canterbury is essential for a proper appreciation of their meaning. From Norman times till the reign of Henry VIII it was served by Benedictine monks; the early Perpendicular cloister walks, some Norman buildings, a conduit tower, and some other structures still remind us of the great domestic establishment needed by so large and flourishing a community.

The pre-Conquest cathedral was of some size and splendour. But it has disappeared, and its successor, built by Archbishop Lanfranc (1070–89) has suffered almost as much; some work in the western transepts alone outlasted the destruction, in the 1830's, of its north-western tower. Twelfth-century Norman work remains, in the eastern limb, in the magnificent crypt, in the outer walls and eastern transepts, and in the turrets which flanked the apse of 'Conrad's Glorious Choir'. In one of these turrets the chapel of St. Anselm retains, in a corner which escaped the flames of 1174, the twelfth-century

58

23   *Canterbury retrochoir: a window of the early thirteenth cent*

24   *The choir screen; western frontage, c. 1400*

wall painting, of St. Paul shaking off the adder, which is one of England's loveliest pieces of Romanesque art.

The devastation of 1174 led to the building, inside the walls of the eastern limb, of a new choir, and of a wholly new extension, above its own early Gothic crypt, which ends in the circular 'corona' chapel; this now houses the stone throne, of about 1220, in which the archbishops are enthroned. The body of St. Thomas was now moved from the crypt to the new retrochoir. It was here, till its destruction in 1538, that pilgrims venerated the relics in the gilt and jewelled shrine over the martyred archbishop's remains. The refashioned and enlarged eastern limb was England's first example of true Gothic as this had been evolved in northern France. William of Sens, its designer, modelled his work on the cathedral of his own city, and though the choir at Canterbury suffers, when compared with later French Gothic masterpieces, from its modest internal height it is none the less of extreme architectural importance. Splendid glass of the early thirteenth century

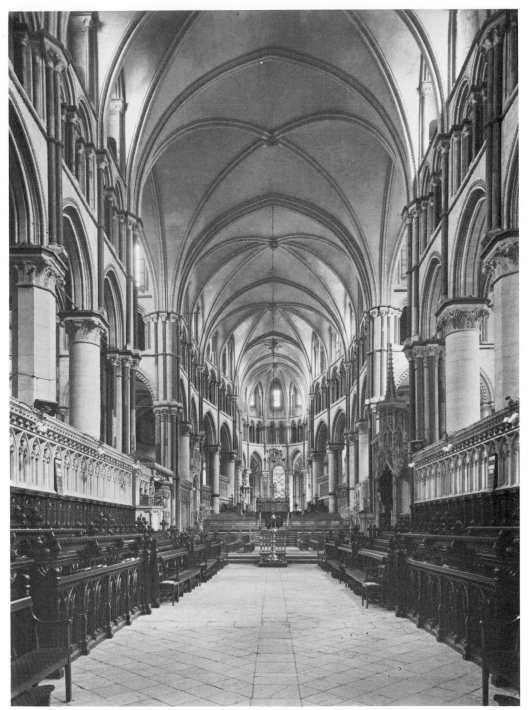

25   *Choir renewed; England's first true Gothic*

survives in some aisle windows, while the still earlier glass from some choir lancets, now in the great window of the south-west transept, is England's finest glass of the twelfth century.

Canterbury is unimportant for 'Decorated' architecture, but late in the fourteenth century work started on the splendid early Perpendicular nave which was in progress when Chaucer wrote his 'Canterbury Tales'. As it covers no more than the site of Lanfranc's modest nave it is short, but the loftiness of its aisles and arcades, and of its central, clerestoried section give it a feeling of height and splendour. The southern porch and the south-west tower are Perpendicular work of the fifteenth century. Late in the same century the magnificent central tower was completed, with its strongly vertical lines and clustered corner pinnacles; its weight soon caused the insertion of the attractive girder arches which grace the nave.

The cathedral is expectedly rich in mediaeval and post-Reformation tombs and memorials. Historically the most important are the two which once flanked Becket's shrine—those of the Black Prince and his nephew King Henry IV. Of archiepiscopal tombs two of the fifteenth century, of Archbishop Chicheley and Cardinal Kemp, are of special splendour. Down in the nave the Carolean font is in the Renaissance taste, while in the choir the fine Restoration Baroque return stalls hint at the sober splendour of many cathedral choirs as restored after Puritan wrecking.

27   The tomb of the Black Prince, d. 1376

Carlisle

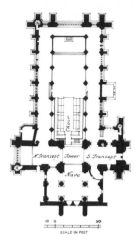

The diocese of Carlisle, created in 1133, was the last of England's pre-Reformation bishoprics. Its cathedral church had already been built as that of a priory of Augustinian regular canons who continued to serve the cathedral—the only one in England to have an Augustinian Chapter.

The original church was in a sturdy, simple, Norman style, of modest size when compared with the more ambitious churches of the great Benedictine monasteries. Of this church the survivals are the crossing piers (with later arches above them) and the two eastern bays of what was originally a full-length nave. The rest of this nave was destroyed during the Civil War. Despite various projects the destroyed portion was never rebuilt, and the surviving bays have, in recent years, been beautifully fitted up as the war memorial chapel of the Border Regiment.

The architectural glory of Carlisle Cathedral lies in its ambitious eastern limb, put up on a cathedralesque scale to fit the status of the church after the changes of 1133. It was first built in the Early English style of the thirteenth century, and as it was planned to be wider than the older nave and crossing it is not, on its northern side, aligned with the North aisle of the nave, or with the northern crossing arch which now, with the aid of a fifteenth-century 'strainer' arch, helps to support the modest Perpendicular central tower. The choir limb was ravaged by fire in 1292. But, except for its eastern bay which was added in the fourteenth century, the present choir retains the arcades (with capitals beautifully recarved in the fourteenth century), and the vaulting

64

and outer aisle walls of the Early English work. The choir was lengthened by one bay, and its upper structure was renewed, in the 'Decorated' style. The nine-light East window, with its superb display of curvilinear tracery, is the most beautiful East window in any English cathedral; like that at Bristol it has fine original glass in its tracery lights. The choir is unvaulted, but has an impressive wooden barrel roof.

Carlisle Cathedral is well off for old fittings and furnishings. The canopied choir stalls, backed by contemporary paintings of the lives of St. Cuthbert, St. Anthony Abbot, and St. Augustine of Hippo, are admirable late mediaeval woodwork. More interesting, and the best early Renaissance screenwork in any English cathedral, is the screen set up, about 1542, by Dean Salkeld who had been the last Augustinian cathedral prior; it well symbolises the transition from the old ecclesiastical order to the new. The tombs and later monuments are of no great note, but two brasses of bishops are important. The canopied

28   *Transepts, tower and truncated nave*

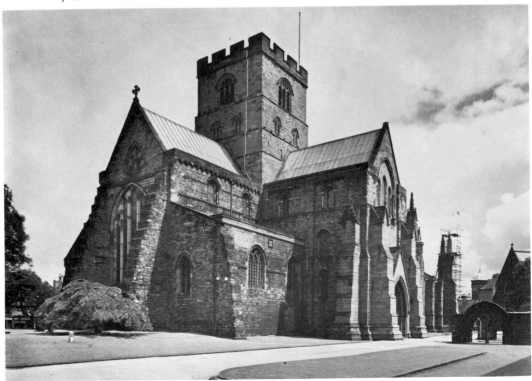

one of Bishop Bell (d. 1496) is one of the country's best episcopal brasses, while the elaborately engraved plate to Bishop Robinson (d. 1616) is a copy of one in the chapel of Queen's College, Oxford of which the bishop, a Cumbrian like many other Queen's men, was Provost in plurality with his poorly endowed see.

29　The choir: early Gothic arches, Decorated East window

Chester

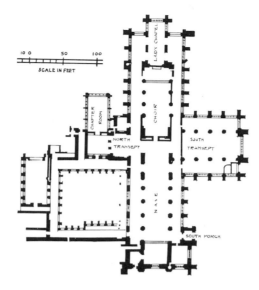

The cathedral at Chester is another of those whose dioceses were created by Henry VIII. Cheshire and Lancashire were taken from the large diocese of Lichfield, and the Benedictine abbey church of St. Werburga at Chester became a cathedral; many of the domestic buildings, including the cloister walks, the Chapter House, and the fine thirteenth-century refectory with its wall pulpit, were fortunately preserved to serve the needs of the new Chapter and its cathedral school.

The abbey, succeeding a pre-Conquest foundation of secular clergy, was founded in 1093 by Hugh Lupus, Earl of Chester. The main structure of the small North transept, and one bay of the northern nave arcade, remain from the Norman church; the rest of the building was replaced, at various times, by Gothic work. A special feature, whose great size comes from its having served as St. Oswald's parish church, is the fourteenth-century South transept which is the largest transept in any English cathedral.

The Early English Lady Chapel, like that built later at Exeter Cathedral, was at first a separate building. Its junction with the present choir was part of a long process of rebuilding and extension started late in the thirteenth century, and completed, with appropriate window tracery, in the 'Decorated' period. The sturdy Perpendicular central tower, with its battlemented corner turrets renewed last century, was erected late in the fifteenth century. Much of the

67

30   South-eastern aspect, with the giant South transept

cathedral's red sandstone masonry has had to be renewed, while a prominent, hideous piece of Victorian building is the tall 'candle snuffer' roof which Scott placed over the south-eastern chapel of the choir. The replacement of the Norman nave, with no triforium and with acutely pointed arches sympathetic to those of the eastern limb, was carried out in the Perpendicular style, the western end and the West front being more typically early Tudor.

The shrine of the Mercian princess St. Werburga, a two-tiered work of ornamental stonework in the Decorated style, now stands near the entrance to the Lady Chapel. More splendid, of about 1390, are the canopied choir stalls which can fairly be claimed as the finest set in the country. They were a model for those, of the same century, in the Cheshire parish church of Nantwich, and for the modern stalls at Downside Abbey. Some good Baroque mural monuments are mostly of the seventeenth century, while the large black marble bowl font was made about 1700.

In the choir:
of the late
eenth century

Chichester

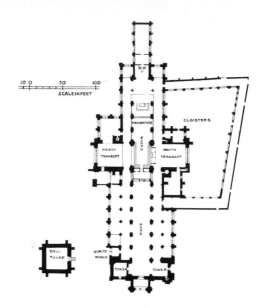

SCALE IN FEET

The cathedral of the ancient Sussex bishopric was long at Selsey, on a site eventually inundated by the sea. In 1075, as part of a general policy whereby all cathedrals were to be in fortified towns, it was moved a few miles inland to Chichester. It is the only one of England's mediaeval cathedrals visible from the sea. It was always a secular foundation, and as both bishopric and chapter were modestly endowed it remained, in essence, the Romanesque cathedral begun in the 1090's. Though its ornament is sparing it has many points of interest and, like all our cathedrals, is in some respects unique. It alone, of all English cathedrals, retains its detached belfry, an imposing tower of the Perpendicular period.

The nave, transepts, and most of the choir limb are those of the Norman cathedral, but soon before 1200, at a time of early Gothic remodelling, the nave and choir were given a simple ribbed vault, moulded inner arches, and Purbeck marble shafts. More important, and replacing the apsidal East end, was the brilliant early Gothic work of the square-ended retrochoir which connects with a Norman eastern chapel refashioned at this time and lengthened, about 1300, as a Lady Chapel. The retrochoir, with arches still rounded and early foliate capitals, has rightly been compared with Canterbury Cathedral's eastern limb.

The central tower was built in the thirteenth century and the spire a century

70

Chichester: the cathedral, with its separate belfry, from the South

later; both were replaced, after collapsing in 1861, in an almost exact copy by Scott. Chapels off the nave aisles, added at various thirteenth-century dates, make Chichester's nave the widest in any English cathedral. Some of the

cathedral's windows are Perpendicular, but this late Gothic period was more important for various furnishings, and for early Renaissance paintings in the transepts or on the choir vault.

The Romanesque sculptured panels, moving and vigorous and once considered to be Saxon, are now attributed to the twelfth century. Chichester Cathedral is fairly rich in mediaeval tombs, while several later memorials, including seven by Flaxman, are to people who touched history at many points; the most notable is to the statesman William Huskisson who was Chichester's M.P. and who, in 1830, was accidentally killed at the opening of the Liverpool to Manchester Railway. Two splendid brass chandeliers are of 1752, while two important changes have lately affected the choir. The stone screen put up by Bishop Arundell (1459–77) has been reinstated across the nave's eastern bay, while a modern reredos has made way, in a cathedral lately notable for its patronage of contemporary artists, for a striking tapestry by John Piper.

34 *Norman nave and Bishop Arundell's screen*   35 *The presbytery and John Piper's tapestry*

Durham

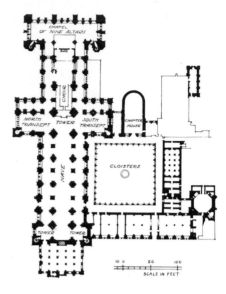

The location of the Northumbrian bishop's headquarters was closely linked to the whereabouts of the body of St. Cuthbert (d. 687). After varied wanderings the saint found a final resting place in the easily fortified position of Durham, high above the Wear in that river's dramatic loop. There, from the Norman period, one had the combination of a strong castle and of the greatest, most innovating in its structure, of England's Romanesque cathedrals which was served, till the sixteenth century, by Benedictine monks. The mediaeval diocese, whose bishops were secular counts palatine as well as being spiritual superiors, included both Northumberland and Co. Durham.

The Saxon cathedral was replaced by the great Norman Romanesque church whose structure and decoration place it high among the masterpieces of European architecture. Not all of it is Norman work, and its far-seen, unpinnacled central tower is a severe achievement in the Perpendicular style. But, with many changes in its window design, and some 're-Normanisation' of windows by Scott, it remains, in essence, a great church of the eleventh and twelfth centuries.

The choir limb, whose eastern bay and vault are now Early English, is the oldest part of the Norman cathedral. The transepts and the nave followed by about 1133. The innovating point in the design was that the *whole* church, and not merely its aisles, was always meant to be covered by a simple *rib* vault.

74

37 *The chapel of the Nine Altars, thirteenth century*

38 *Romanesque setting, Carolean Gothic; Bishop Cosin's font and its arcaded canopy*

The great cross arches, as one still sees in the nave, were pointed in the manner of the Gothic style which followed. The construction of the great church is even more remarkable than its scale and grandeur and the varied decoration of the pillars which was copied in some other churches. A later Romanesque work, somewhat backward for its date of about 1175 which is also that of the early Gothic choir at Canterbury, is the five-aisled 'Galilee' chapel, with round-arched arcades and lavish chevron moulding, which was added to the earlier West end.

At each end Durham Cathedral has important work of the thirteenth century. The two western towers are largely of this period, while the original apse was replaced, in a mixture of lancet and geometrical Gothic, by the eastern bay of the presbytery and by the great eastern transept with its nine small chapels. Its rose window is by Wyatt, replacing a somewhat similar window from long before his time.

The shrine of St. Cuthbert stood on one side of the eastern transept, being parted from the presbytery by the delicate, beautifully pinnacled altar screen given, about 1372, by Lord Neville of Raby. A striking feature of the choir is Bishop Hatfield's tomb of about 1375; it is ingeniously worked into a single composition with the double stairway and canopy of the episcopal throne.

The choir at Durham was ravaged by Scots prisoners confined there in 1650. Bishop Cosin's canopied stalls of the 1660's are like his splendid font canopy in that they combine a basically late Gothic design with some Renaissance detail.

There are substantial remains of the monastic buildings, including a simple Norman undercroft, the famous octagonal vaulted kitchen, and the dormitory which, for easier drainage down to the river, is on the cloisters' western side.

Ely

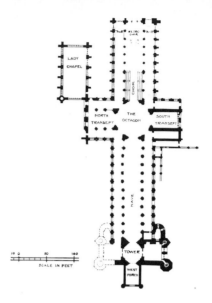

The diocese of Ely was created, in 1109, as a first attempt to diminish the unduly large diocese of Lincoln. The Benedictine abbey, of pre-Conquest origins but imposingly rebuilt since 1066, became a cathedral served by monks till the Dissolution in 1539; as in other similar cases the last prior became the first dean. The monastic buildings suffered severely, but there are important remains of the great aisled infirmary and of the prior's house (later the deanery) with a charming sexfoil window in its western gable, while the adjoining chapel built by Prior Crauden is a most attractive building of the fourteenth century.

The great Norman abbey church was started, about 1085, by Abbot Simeon who had been prior at Winchester. The design of the transepts was certainly worked out in his time, and there are strong resemblances between them and the Norman transepts at Winchester. Little survives of the fairly long eastern limb, but the Norman work west of the crossing is among the masterpieces of European Romanesque. The nave, with alternately rounded and clustered pillars, simple cushion capitals, and a lofty triforium stage now lit by rows of Perpendicular windows, was finished after the church became a cathedral and is covered by a timber ceiling whose present structure and paintings are Victorian. The severity of the nave is relieved, outside, by the splendidly decorative prior's door, with Christ in Glory in its sculptured

78

40   *In the Octagon, timber vault and upper lantern*

tympanum. The nave ends in a western composition whose original design, a richly arcaded tower flanked by boldly turretted transepts, made it uniquely imposing. But the symmetry of this magnificent *Westwerk* suffered when its northern transept almost wholly collapsed. The grouping was originally finished late in the twelfth century, and the main external arches on the tower, and high up in the wall arcading, are slightly pointed. The 'Galilee' western porch dates from the thirteenth century, with lancets and rich wall arcading.

The next important work, beginning Ely's fine contrast between Romanesque and Gothic, was the ornately Early English retrochoir, built about 1230–52 to house St. Etheldreda's shrine. The new building was given an impressive East end, with lancet windows and early tracery in its triforium arches.

A chapel off the South transept has a geometrical window, but the next great building phase came after 1300. In 1323 the fall of the Norman central tower, and the damage then caused to the presbytery, caused the renewal, in most elaborate 'Decorated', of the western portion of the eastern limb; this had, like the nave and transepts, been shortened by one bay when Prior Alan of Walsingham, with William Hurley as his master carpenter, opened out the crossing into the great octagon whose wooden vault supports the timber lantern tower. This central octagon is unique in any English cathedral and may well have inspired Wren's pre-Fire scheme for a domed octagon at Old St. Paul's. Next came the completion of the Lady Chapel, unusually wide with a rich lierne vault and a wealth of niches and sculpture, a 'Decorated' masterpiece but in some of its windows anticipating 'Perpendicular'; as at Peterborough it was sited north-east of the North transept.

41   Decorated detail, arcading in the Lady Chapel

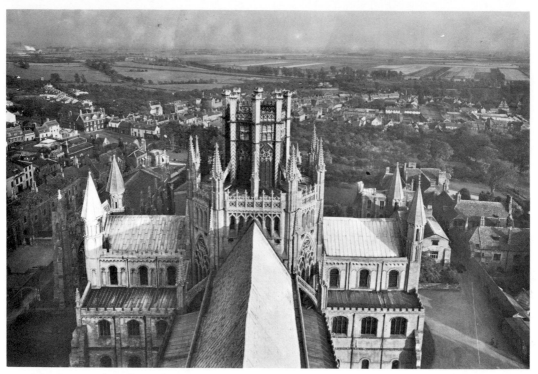

The last important structural addition was the early Perpendicular top stage of the western tower. The older tower's great Transitional Norman arches, slightly pointed and with two courses of moulded zig-zag decoration, had to be strengthened by inner arches. In the transepts the hammerbeam roofs, and the varied windows of the main walls, are of the fifteenth century.

Despite heavy Victorian refurnishing the choir stalls are still mostly the canopied set of the fourteenth century, while the cathedral is notable for the fine free-standing tombs, several of them richly canopied, of various bishops. More striking still was refashioning of the two eastern side chapels as the chantries of Bishops Alcock (d. 1500) and West (d. 1533). Both display extremely rich late Perpendicular work, and the West chantry has some Renaissance decoration. The cathedral is also remarkable for two Baroque doorways, said to be by Wren but more probably designed by Robert Grumbold of Cambridge.

Exeter

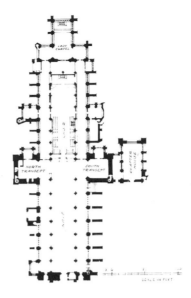

The Devon bishopric was created, along with that of Somerset, when the large Wessex diocese of Sherborne was split up in 909. The Cornish see, with its headquarters at St. German's, was founded a little later, but in the 1040's the two were merged, with the bishop's seat at Crediton. Then in 1050, in an anticipation under Edward the Confessor of what happened more widely under the Normans, the throne was moved to the fortified city of Exeter. What had been the church of a Benedictine monastery became a cathedral; it was soon turned over to secular canons and Exeter, with the residences of its clergy well dispersed and Calendarhay the equivalent of the Vicars' Closes of some other cathedrals, remained a 'secular' foundation.

The flanking towers of Bishop Warelwast's Norman cathedral, planned in the Rhenish manner and pinnacled much later, gave Exeter Cathedral its distinctive and much loved silhouette. They are the best, but not the only survivals of the Norman building. For the aisle walls of the nave, and of part of the choir, are also basically Norman, though with 'Decorated' windows, while the bomb hit of 1942 revealed that much Norman stonework was re-used as the rubble core of later walling.

The cathedral's century-long transformation started with the building, over the site of the Saxon church, of a fine eastern Lady Chapel in the Geometrical idiom; like some others it was originally a separate structure. The filling of the space between that chapel and the eastern apse of the Norman church, and the replacement of the older eastern limb, gave Exeter its long and splendid choir, while the position of the towers allowed for the roof, over 300 feet long, which is the longest unbroken roof over any English cathedral. From the choir westwards this was the process, under Bishops Quivil, Bitton, Stapledon, and Grandisson, which gave Exeter, with its

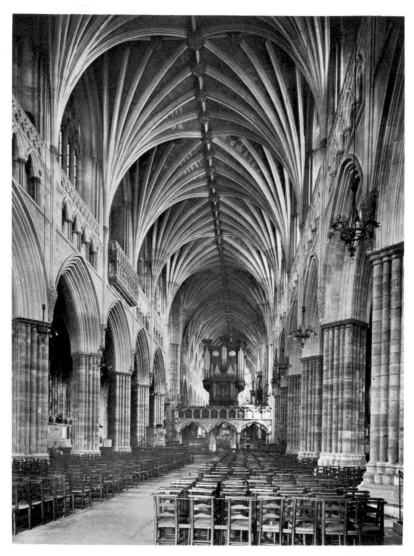

43 *The nave looking through to the choir, fourteenth century*

44　*The tomb of Bishop Stafford, d. 1419*

clustered pillars, rich tierceron vault, ornate bosses and corbels, and varied tracery, the feeling of a cathedral more completely in the 'Decorated' style than all others in England. The choir, with its East window altered to early Perpendicular, is specially fine, but when in the 1360's the nave was finished, and was given the screen, with its niches and statues, across the western façade, the 'Decorated' style was outdated. Chantries and tombs apart, not much of the cathedral is 'Perpendicular'.

The stone choir screen, supporting the organ in its fine Restoration case, is a delicately ornamented work of the fourteenth century. Most of the choir fittings are Victorian, but in the stalls the seats, with misericords, are of about 1260 and are the oldest set in England. The throne, whose rich canopy rises nearly 60 feet, is a superb piece of mediaeval woodwork and was in progress in 1316; it is the country's finest episcopal throne. The cathedral has a fair wealth of fourteenth-century glass, and among its rare treasures is a mediaeval 'orrery' clock.

Exeter is rich in the tombs of bishops and cathedral clergy, and of mediaeval and more recent Devon worthies. Its most beautiful post-Reformation fitting is the canopied marble font, a Baroque gem of 1684.

Gloucester

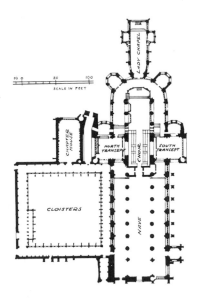

As a work of architecture the cathedral at Gloucester is, perhaps, the most important of the abbey churches which escaped destruction by being made cathedrals under Henry VIII. More than once it was the scene of pioneering moves in design. Its origins go back to about 680 when Osric, the 'sub-king' of south-western Mercia, founded a 'minster' for monks and nuns. His tomb, showing him in royal garb, was set up about 1520. After a chequered Anglo-Saxon career his religious house settled down, under the able Norman abbot Serlo, as the greatest of many Benedictine monasteries in the lower Severn basin. In 1541 it became the cathedral of most of its own county.

The oldest part of the church is the early Norman crypt, with short columns in its central portion and radiating chapels whose plan is repeated off the choir aisles and triforium. In the presbytery the stumpy cylindrical columns with their low arches contrast with the tall pillars and richer arches of the nave arcades. Two Norman western towers were replaced when, in the fifteenth century, the church's western end was rebuilt. The wooden roof of the nave was replaced, as a fire precaution, by the somewhat heavy stone thirteenth-century vault.

The church's great transformation started, soon after 1300, with the remodelling of the nave's South aisle where the 'Decorated' windows have a lavish display of ballflower ornament. The refashioning of the transepts and

87

Flanking towers are the distinctive feature at Exeter

47 *A choir transformed, Norman and early Perpendicular*   48 *The Lady Chapel, Perpendicular of c. 1480*

presbytery followed in the 30 years after 1330. The basic structure of the Romanesque church was retained, but the inner walls were cased with a delicate, cage-like complex of mullions and tracery which is the earliest important Perpendicular work to have survived. It combined with the enormous new East window, the new clerestorey, and a richly bossed lierne vault to give the feeling of a sumptuous memorial chapel to the murdered king Edward II whose marvellously canopied tomb lies under a Norman arch. Gloucester's other royal tomb, that of Robert of Normandy, is in the middle of the choir.

89

Norman nave, vault thirteenth century

49 Gloucester Lady Chapel: varied monuments, Elizabethan and Georgian Baroque

50 Gloucester cloisters: the lavatorium, early fan v

Before 1400 another significant piece of architecture had probably been started. The fan vaulting of Gloucester's cloister walks may not, in relation to that of the Chapter House at Hereford, have been England's earliest fan vault. It is, however, the earliest still standing; the whole cloister, with its *lavatorium* and recesses for monks' desks, is of admirable distinction.

The fifteenth century saw the building of the elaborately pinnacled central tower and the masonry struts, some of them unattractive in their interior effect, needed to support its great weight. The abbey's final addition, about 1480, was the magnificent Lady Chapel, the finest in England in the Perpendicular style.

Royalty apart, Gloucester Cathedral is rich in mediaeval tombs and in Renaissance, Baroque, and later Georgian monuments to local and county magnates. The fine canopied choir stalls are of the fifteenth century, while the East window is filled with glass, of about 1350, in silver, blue and red; among its small figures is one of a man playing a game like hockey.

51 *King Edward II, d. 1327*

Hereford

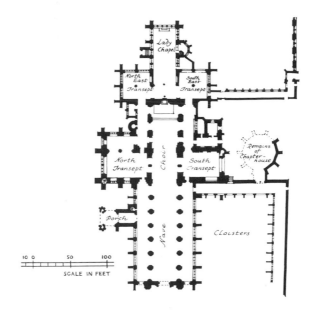

The diocese, once including West Gloucestershire as well as Herefordshire and southern Shropshire, was one of those created, about 680, to relieve that of Lichfield. It had in the Middle Ages a secular Chapter, and as this and the bishopric were modestly endowed the cathedral remained, in essence, a Romanesque building, but with many alterations and additions making it varied, lovable, and of great interest. It is of modest size, and its nave is one bay shorter than it was before the West end collapsed in 1786.

The present cathedral was started by Bishop Robert 'of Lotharingia'; the eastern ends of its choir aisles were once capped by the Rhenish feature of flanking towers. The South transept has, on its eastern wall, a fine grouping of blind arches and arcading. The choir, though now without its apse and with an Early English upper stage, is still, in the main, an unlengthened Norman building. The fine eastern Lady Chapel, above its vaulted crypt, is early thirteenth century; it is the oldest of such buildings in any English cathedral. The retrochoir and its chapels blend Transitional Norman and 'Decorated' work.

Between 1250 and 1270 a new North transept, Geometrical, blending French and English influences, and of outstanding excellence, was built by Bishop Aquablanca. Apart from many aisle windows the cathedral's best 'Decorated' work is the central tower with its tall windows and ballflower ornament. The western tower which fell in 1786 was also of this period. Various windows, and such small additions as the Stanbury and Audley chantries, and the graceful outer North porch of Bishop Booth (1516–35) were the chief Perpendicular contributions. The nave arcades are still Norman,

52 *The main fabric is seen from across the Close*

Punning detail from the tomb of Canon John de Swinfield

54   *In the Chained Library*

but everything above them is dignified Gothic work, in the fourteenth-century manner, by James Wyatt whose West front was replaced, in 1904–08, by Oldrid Scott's ornate Gothic composition.

The cathedral's contents are of great note; it is, among other points, England's best cathedral for brasses. Its mediaeval tombs are admirable; outstanding among them, and our earliest of its type, is the free-standing tomb, with a lovely 'Geometrical' canopy, of Bishop Aquablanca. The chained library, and the *Mappa Mundi* of about 1290, are treasures of international fame. The canopied throne is of the fourteenth century; an even more important piece of furniture is the chair, almost certainly from before 1138 when King Stephen is said to have sat in it.

The fan-vaulted Chapter House is almost wholly ruined. But Norman timber arches survive in the Palace, and Vicars' Close, a square quadrangle of the fifteenth century, is of the utmost charm.

95

Lichfield

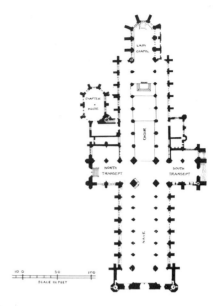

As a diocesan centre Lichfield has had a most varied history. Under St. Chad (699–672) who made it his headquarters the diocese included the whole of Mercia, but other bishoprics, such as Worcester and Hereford, were later created to reduce its inconvenient size. Late in the eighth century, when King Offa of Mercia was the leading figure in Anglo-Saxon England, Lichfield was briefly made the seat of an archbishop. After temporary Norman moves to Chester and Coventry the diocese, including Cheshire and Lancashire, settled down under the dual title of Coventry and Lichfield. Coventry Cathedral was served by Benedictine monks, with Lichfield a foundation of secular canons.

Of the Norman cathedral nothing remains above ground, and as in another secular cathedral, at Wells, the oldest work at Lichfield is Early English Gothic, though little remains of the original fenestration. The choir arches date from just before 1200. The single-aisled transepts, the fine crossing arches, and the lower part of the central tower are of the thirteenth century. So too is the Chapter House, an attractive building designed, with vaulting and a central pillar, as an elongated octagon.

The nave, of the second half of the thirteenth century, is excellent 'Geometrical' Gothic with the rarity of a clerestorey of convex-sided triangular windows. As at Lincoln and Wells the West front, with its three doorways,

and tiers of canopied recesses now containing Victorian statues, was planned as a splendid screen to the nave; its fourteenth-century stonework suffered so much from the weather, and from windborne pollution from the Black Country, that it was almost wholly renewed, from 1856 onwards, by Scott. The two western spires are still, for the most part, fourteenth-century work; along with the central spire which had to be replaced after the Civil War, they give Lichfield its famous three-spired silhouette, now unique among England's mediaeval cathedrals.

Lichfield's most notable work is at the eastern end; the choir limb's architectural evolution much resembled that of Wells. The early Decorated Lady Chapel, like Lichfield's Chapter House an elongated octagon, was originally a separate building nearly as lofty as the choir. A little later in the fourteenth century the master mason William Ramsey lengthened the choir, demolished the Lady Chapel's eastern end, and cleverly made a unified composition,

G

without a triforium stage, of almost the entire eastern limb. Most of his fine Decorated windows were replaced by the Perpendicular windows which still light the choir, but his clerestorey splays still have their rare, attractive decoration of quatrefoil panelling.

Lichfield Cathedral is not outstanding for its mediaeval tombs, and the 'Grecian' Chantrey, with two important monuments, is better represented than Renaissance or Georgian sculptors. The fittings and furnishing are nearly all Victorian, but in the Lady Chapel the splendid glass of the 1530's which was, before the French Revolution, in the Cistercian nuns' church of Herkenrode near Liège is the finest Continental glass in any English cathedral.

57   *The choir, looking through to the Lady Chapel*

Lincoln

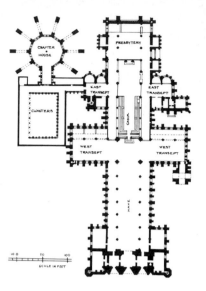

The great cathedral at Lincoln was built as the headquarters of a diocese stretching across the eastern Midlands from the Humber to the Thames. After various moves, the Saxon bishops' final seat was at Dorchester in Oxfordshire. Remigius, the first post-Conquest bishop, soon moved to the fortified, but hardly more central city of Lincoln. He also established the secular Chapter which from then onwards served the cathedral.

Of the Norman cathedral built by Remigius, and more elaborately adorned by Bishop Alexander the Magnificent (1123–48) the only remains are in the lower parts of the West front and of the two towers above it. The replacement of the Norman cathedral started under St. Hugh (1186–1200) whose pioneering, not wholly attractive early Gothic choir and eastern transepts are contemporary with the earliest Gothic work at Wells. The thirteenth-century central transepts gave Lincoln, alone among English cathedrals, two large circular windows. 'The Dean's Eye', with early Geometrical tracery, has splendid contemporary glass. 'The Bishop's Eye' in the South transept, has exquisite tracery of the following century.

The nave, with large chapels leading off its aisles, was designed by the master mason Alexander and built in the mature Early English style. It is the finest nave in that idiom, and the ten-sided Chapter House is of about the same date. Less happy, and spreading above and to each side of the Norman

58 Romanesque West portal, statues above late fourteenth cen

façade, is the sprawling, arcaded thirteenth-century addition to the West
front. Much finer work was started, about 1255, when the 'Angel' choir was
added, at the cathedral's other end, to house St. Hugh's shrine. The eastern
part of the saint's choir was destroyed; the resulting building, with a great
East window and rich sculptured detail, is the best 'Geometrical' achievement
in any English cathedral.

Henceforward, little was added to the cathedral's ground area. The upper
part of the central tower, making it the highest above any cathedral in England,
is early 'Decorated', while the upper stages of the western towers are from the
late fourteenth century. All three towers once had spires, the two western
ones lasting till 1807.

The choir has very fine canopied stalls of about 1370, but the throne and
altarpiece are interesting Georgian Gothic work by James Essex of Cambridge.
Some mediaeval tombs and chantries survive, but the Puritans destroyed
dozens of brasses. Among the cathedral's attendant buildings the classical

102

library of 1674 is Wren's only building for a cathedral outside London,
while the West end of the nave has the rarity, for a mediaeval church, of some
architectural work by Gibbs.

London

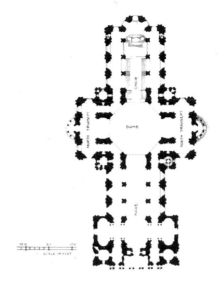

The diocese of London, like that of Rochester, was founded very early in the seventh century. Its existence, and the presence of a cathedral on the site of St. Paul's, have been continuous, and the Pre-Reformation cathedral had a secular Chapter. Where the present cathedral is unique in England is that, thanks to the destruction of its Norman and Gothic predecessor in 1666, it is wholly in a Renaissance style. But its plan was much influenced by those of Old St. Paul's, and of other elongated cathedrals like Lincoln, whose nave chapels are the equivalent of the chapels off the nave aisles of Wren's St. Paul's.

Despite a scheme to recondition the nave of the gutted cathedral the main fabric of the present St. Paul's is an entirely new building; some buttress foundations of the fourteenth century Chapter House are the only above-ground remains of the earlier cathedral.

Even after the rejection of Wren's favoured 'Model' design, allowing for the main body of the cathedral on a Greek cross plan, many design alterations occurred before the new cathedral was complete. What Londoners got by 1710 was very different from what had been approved in the 'Warrant' design of 1675. The plan of the present cathedral, with its long choir limb, was conditioned by the desire of the clergy for a cathedral, with a screened off choir of mediaeval dimensions to which they had, in various places, become accustomed. The resulting church was a somewhat uneasy com-

62　*The dome, and the whole southern side of Wren's St. Paul's*

promise between a mediaeval cathedral in Renaissance dress and the domed Renaissance church, with its short sanctuary and 'Jesuit' planning, more normal in Counter-Reformation Europe.

Wren's St. Paul's is cruciform, with the lantern above its dome supported by a hidden cone of brick and in its basic idea fulfilling Wren's project for a domed St. Paul's. The screen walls which mask the clerestorey make the church look larger than it is, but its scale is most grand and its Portland stone masonry is highly impressive. The crypt, with its central cluster of Roman Doric pillars and simple piers below the nave and choir, extends (unlike mediaeval crypts) below the cathedral's full length. The choir walls and the imposing East end were started in 1675. The transepts, with sculptured pediments and curved porches, followed, and very soon the nave with its western vestibule, side chapels below the Library and the 'model' room, and the two-tiered West front. Throughout the upper structure the Corinthian and 'composite' orders are used. The design of the building, and the processes of its erection, are better documented than for any pre-Reformation cathedral.

Wren's greatest departures from his original designs were in the dome and in the two western turrets. As first planned, the turrets were much simpler than the splendidly Roman Baroque pair now above the West front. The great dome, with its colonnaded drum, leaded outer structure, and well-proportioned lantern was the final result of an often changing process of design.

The space beneath the dome, performing for St. Paul's what the Octagon does for Ely, is easily the most successful part of the interior. The choir, no longer screened from the nave and with its Baroque organ case of William and Mary's reign split between its two sides, now ends in the recent High Altar, with its Berniniesque *baldachino* which fulfils Wren's original idea; behind it is the American Memorial Chapel. Gibbons' carved stalls, and the brilliant Baroque ironwork by the Huguenot, Tijou, are its best furnishings.

Most of the monuments in the upper part of the cathedral are to heroes of the Napoleonic war. The idea of a national Valhalla, with a wider representation including writers, musicians, architects and painters as well as famous fighting men, is continued in the crypt. The simple plaque to Wren, and the monuments of his daughter Jane and other relatives of the great architect, are of outstanding interest. Some damaged Elizabethan and Jacobean effigies remain from Old St. Paul's, but the oldest object in the cathedral is the black

marble sarcophagus, of early sixteenth century Italian Renaissance design,
which was first made for Wolsey, was appropriated by Henry VIII, and now
contains the remains of Nelson.

109

Nelson's tomb in the crypt below the dome

65   *Some of Gibbons' stalls in the choir*

Norwich

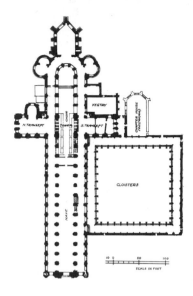

The cathedral of the Saxon bishops of East Anglia was long at North Elmham in central Norfolk. But after a short post-Conquest spell at Thetford the see was moved to Norwich where, in 1096, Bishop Herbert de Losinga started a cathedral whose eastern end covered the site of a much older chapel. A Benedictine monastery served it; of this the main survivals are the beautifully vaulted cloisters, partly 'Decorated' and in part early Perpendicular, and the Prior's doorway which is, with canopied figures superimposed on its mouldings, a fine work of the East Anglian sculptural school. The precincts are finely approached by the Ethelbert and Erpingham Gates, the former of about 1300, the latter some 120 years later.

Despite many Gothic embellishments Norwich is still a great periapsidal Romanesque cathedral, with its fifteenth-century stone spire rising above the best Norman central tower of any English cathedral. The presbytery's side arches were much altered about 1500, but two tiers of the Norman apse arches remain finely intact. The original bishop's throne, here as in no other English cathedral, is under the apse's central arch—the position normal in early basilican cathedrals. The monastic subdivision—nave, a choir West of and under the tower, and presbytery—survives admirably at Norwich, while the structural nave, very long and with its seven double bays perhaps meant to have a stone vault, is mainly Romanesque. The clerestorey of the presbytery

67 *In the Norman ambulatory*   68 *A cloister walk, fourteenth century*

was renewed after 1362, and well shows the transition from 'Decorated' to Perpendicular. But here, as in the transepts and nave, the vault is a splendid, richly bossed one of the late Perpendicular period.

The canopied choir stalls are fine furnishing of the fifteenth century. Norwich Cathedral is not outstandingly rich in mediaeval tombs, but those of the post-Reformation period, including Baroque murals and Georgian work by the local sculptor John Ivory, are of some merit and interest. Some wall paintings of about 1300 are on part of the Norman vault in the North aisle of the presbytery. More important, of the late fourteenth century and fine work of the highly competent East Anglian school of painters, are the two retables, or altar pieces, and various other panels now seen in the chapels of St. Saviour and St. Luke.

113

'n the presbytery, Norman apse, late Gothic upper stage

Oxford

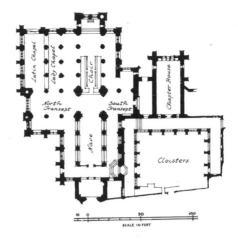

The cathedral at Oxford, the smallest in England, is laid out on the cruciform plan normal in 'greater' abbey or collegiate churches. It well proves that modest size is, in such a building, no bar to great architectural quality. Its nave was at one time considerably longer, and on two occasions this exquisite church at St. Frideswide's Augustinian priory escaped possible destruction. For when in 1524 Wolsey dissolved the priory to make way for Cardinal College he planned a vast new chapel like that of King's at Cambridge, and then when in 1542 Henry VIII carved the Oxford diocese out of that of Lincoln the chief, and perhaps in time the only cathedral was to be the large dissolved abbey church of Osney. But eventually, with Cardinal College refounded as Christ Church the priory church, whose nave had been docked to build one side of Tom Quad, settled down as a cathedral and also, uniquely in England, as a College chapel.

Of the Norman priory the best remains are the ornate main doorway and part of the Chapter House. But most of the church—crossing, transepts, eastern limb, and slightly later nave—is Transitional Norman work started about 1170. The foliate capitals resemble those at Canterbury. More unusual is the device whereby some triforium arcading is squeezed between the tops of the round-headed aisle arches and the loftier, moulded blind arches which spring from the capitals of the pillars; the same feature, larger and with pointed

115

arches was used at Glastonbury Abbey. The choir's eastern bay projects, unaisled, in a typically Augustinian manner; its main wall, once containing a large 'Decorated' window, was unconvincingly re-Normanised by Scott. The upper part of the tower and the ribbed spire are early thirteenth-century— the country's oldest cathedral tower and spire. North of the choir, the Lady Chapel has a beautiful Early English arcade, while beyond it the 'Latin' (St. Catherine's) chapel is good 'Decorated' work. With its old glass and stalls, tombs and monuments, and its late mediaeval tomb supporting a wooden chantry chapel, it is one of the most delectable spots even among the many delights of Oxford.

The choir and nave have a splendid late Perpendicular lierne vault, with partly hidden cross arches and traceried pendents. Had Wolsey not intervened, the transepts would have been similarly covered.

Despite some ponderous Victorian refurnishing, Christ Church Cathedral has many notable contents. Windows by the Flemish van Linge brothers are from Oxford's great Laudian period, while the remains of St. Frideswide's shrine are of about 1290. Post-Reformation monuments, beautifully maintained, commemorate Stuart nobility, eminent Christ Church men, and Dean (also Bishop) John Fell (d. 1686), understandably disliked for his over-dominant position in Restoration Oxford.

71 Nave and choir transitional Norman, vaulting, c. 1500

Peterborough

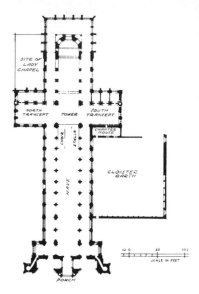

The great Benedictine abbey church at Peterborough, of Saxon origins but mainly Norman in structure, became a cathedral, with its diocese taken from that of Lincoln and at first including Northamptonshire and Rutland, under Henry VIII. It well shows that the pre-Reformation cathedrals had no monopoly of size and architectural splendour.

The present church was started about 1118, and its building took over a hundred years. Despite some later work, and the reconstruction of its windows or the filling of their spaces with tracery, the building is essentially a superb Norman Romanesque church. Even the central tower, when replaced in the fourteenth century, remained stocky in the Norman manner. The apsidal presbytery is of more than average length, but the apse's round-arched effect was lost when, in the fourteenth century, its arches were altered and its windows were filled with 'Decorated' tracery. The cathedral's Norman work, with considerable variety in its pillars and triforium arches, is of great solemnity and splendour, the Romanesque effect being increased by the simply designed, primitively painted wooden ceilings of the transepts and nave. Even in the presbytery the vaulted ceiling of about 1400, with ribs and a flat central section, is of wood, not stone.

The nave's western bays are later in character than the rest of the building, and the nave was to have ended in two western towers and a modest *Westwerk*.

72 *At Peterborough: Norman presbytery, windows designs of the fourteenth cen*

73 *South-western aspect; a general view*

Then in the thirteenth century the present stupendous West front was built, with three arcaded gables above cavernous arches. Though its effect suffers from the non-completion of one of the towers behind it, and from the way in which an early Perpendicular porch-cum-chapel has been jammed into its central giant arch, it is the most imposing façade of its date in any English cathedral.

Late in the thirteenth century a large Lady Chapel was built East of the North transept; it was destroyed in 1661. The final work on the great abbey church was the squaring off of its eastern end with the late Perpendicular New Building whose fan vault is akin to that of King's Chapel at Cambridge.

Not much remains of the principal monastic buildings, and the Puritans savagely wrecked the cathedral's interior; the brass eagle lectern is its only good mediaeval fitting. Mere fragments remain of Queen Catherine of Aragon's tomb, and James I had his mother, Mary Queen of Scots, reburied in Westminster Abbey. The Baroque monument of Thomas Deacon (d. 1721) is worth noticing; so too are some early mediaeval abbots' effigies. The choir furnishings are late Victorian, and Pearson's Italianate Gothic *baldachino* is effective in its basilican setting.

120

74   The New Building, c. 1500; fan vaulting probably by John Wa

Ripon

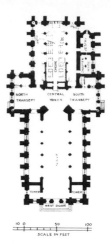

Ripon Cathedral is of Saxon origins, and the simple little crypt, perhaps from the time of St. Wilfrid (c. 670) is the only one of so early a date under any English cathedral. The mediaeval Minster was a great collegiate church in the diocese of York. Its collegiate status was restored, after a gap at the Reformation, under James I. In 1836 it became the cathedral of the first Anglican diocese set up to meet population changes caused by the Industrial Revolution.

Some Norman work remains in the Chapter House's undercroft, but the cathedral's earliest important architecture is 'Transitional' Gothic of about 1190. The nave was at first unusual in being unaisled, and at each end of the present nave triforium and clerestorey stages survive in what were once blank walls. The western façade and towers are in panelled and lancetted Early English, and the older Gothic design is best seen in the North transept. Most of the nave, with aisles and a clerestorey, is now in severe late Perpendicular.

The choir limb is a somewhat puzzling mixture. Behind the fine fifteenth-century screen, with its modern statues, the choir contains work of three different periods—'Transitional' Gothic of about 1190, 'Geometrical' a century later, and Perpendicular rebuilding work caused by the fall, about 1450, of the two sides of the squat central tower; two sides of the present tower are thus late Norman and the other two Perpendicular. Most arches

122

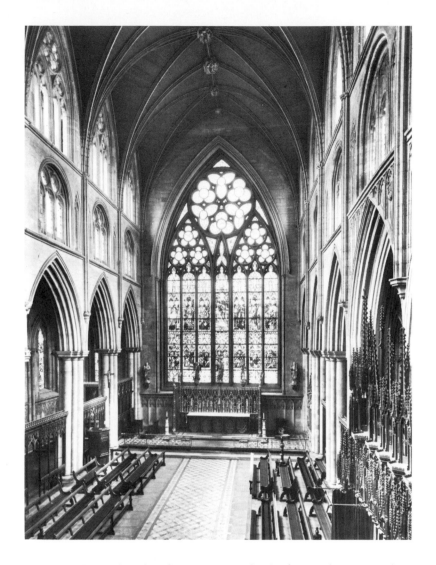

of the choir arcades, and parts of the glazed triforium, are early Gothic with
lingering Romanesque details, while much of the southern side is good late
fifteenth century work replacing what the falling tower destroyed. But the
choir's main glory was the recasting, in fine Geometrical Gothic, of much
of its upper structure, and of its East end where the great seven-light window
is among the finest in that particular style.

76 Choir stalls by local carvers, c. 1500

Some Baroque and later Georgian monuments commemorate Yorkshire gentry, but no furnishing in the cathedral compares with the splendid set of early sixteenth-century choir stalls, the finest in any English cathedral of so late a pre-Reformation date. Some were wrecked when in 1660 the central spire collapsed, and their Carolean replacements were in turn replaced by Scott. Their canopies, their stall ends and misericords, and various other details make them a masterpiece of the local school of woodcarvers.

Rochester

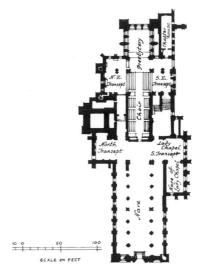

Founded in 604, the see of Rochester is one of England's two oldest after that of Canterbury. With western Kent alone in its diocese, and with the bishopric and the Benedictine cathedral priory slenderly endowed, the historic cathedral remained of a modest size. The monastic buildings, of which there are fairly extensive ruins, were unusual in that they adjoined the choir limb and not the nave.

Foundations of a small Saxon cathedral lie below and west of those of the western façade, but the oldest buildings above ground are the sturdy detached tower and the unpierced side walls of the presbytery, built by the Norman bishop Gundulf (1077–1108). The chief Norman work is, however, in the cathedral's stately nave, most of it built well into the twelfth century. The clerestorey and the timber roof are of about 1500, but most of the arcade arches, and the triforium stage, are splendid Romanesque work, and despite some changes and restoration the façade is the best Norman West front in England.

The cathedral's eastern limb was lengthened, with additional transepts, and its older parts were transformed, in the thirteenth century; they display some excellent Early English work, with lancets, dog-tooth ornament, and dark marble shafts. The crypt accounts for the choir limb's unambitious height (with no triforium), but the thirteenth-century parts of the crypt, vaulted and with many short pillars, make up the best Gothic crypt in the country.

125

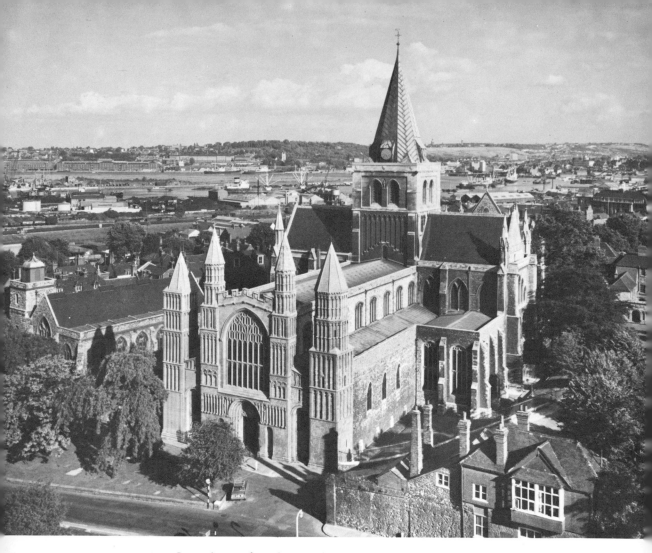

77   *General view, from the castle keep*

The thirteenth-century tower arches support a tower twice renewed in the last 150 years. The present one, whose stumpy spire recalls the mediaeval silhouette, is by the Durham architect Hodgson Fowler. The fourteenth century is best represented by the splendid doorway, with canopied figures round its voussoirs in the French manner, which leads into the Chapter Room.

The Lady Chapel, once also including the south-west transept, is unusually placed off the South nave aisle; it is late Perpendicular and was to have had a fan vault.

Of the few remaining pre-Reformation fittings some thirteenth-century stallwork is the oldest in England, while some mediaeval paintings include, as a rare feature, half of a Wheel of Fortune painted about 1250. Several mediaeval bishops' tombs are of note, particularly the fine effigy and canopy of Bishop John de Sheppey (d. 1360). Among a good group of post-Reformation monuments one by Grinling Gibbons to Sir Richard Head (d. 1689) adds interest to a cathedral which has been underrated, but which is very well worth a visit.

78   *Norman nave: timber roof, c. 1500*

79   *Eastward elongation, Early English, c. 1200*

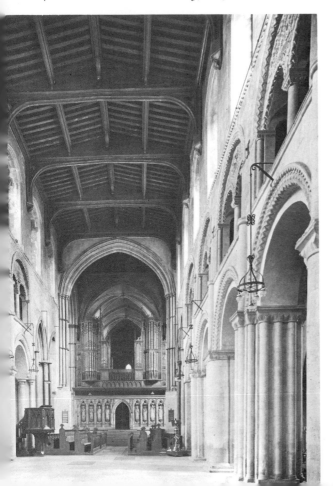

St. Alban's

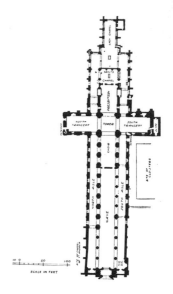

The Benedictine abbey church of St. Alban's was the largest English monastic church which, after the Dissolution of the monasteries, became a parish church. The Lady Chapel was turned into a Grammar School, and the vast remaining fabric was in the end a defeating burden on the parishioners. But in 1877 the church became the cathedral of a new Anglican diocese. Sir Edmund Beckett (later Lord Grimthorpe) then took over the work of restoration begun by Scott, and more so after Scott's death in 1878. He designed and financed almost all that was done. The end walls of the transepts, and the Victorian Geometrical West front which replaced a somewhat bald western end, are due to him. Despite lapses in taste, his money and his restorative efforts may well have saved the cathedral from outright collapse.

The pre-Conquest abbey church was among the first replaced by Norman builders, some turned balusters from its fabric being re-used, in his triforium, by Abbot Paul of Caen who built a severe Norman church with England's most spectacular set of parallel eastern apses. He used much Roman brick from the ruins of Verulamium, and the central tower at St. Alban's is the only one over an English cathedral to be built of brick. Sculpturally unadorned but embellished, on its interior arches, with simple painted geometrical designs, the unaltered Romanesque part of the cathedral is impressively primitive. The twelfth- and thirteenth-century paintings, particularly of Crucifixion

groups, on some of its nave piers are a splendid set and the best mural paintings in any English cathedral. Though of varying dates the timber ceilings of the transepts and nave complete the feeling of early simplicity.

The austerely Early English western part of the nave was added in the thirteenth century, while five of the nave's southern bays had to be rebuilt after a collapse in 1323. The presbytery was somewhat unambitiously recast, with Geometrical windows and a dignified timber vault, not long before 1300. The eastern Lady Chapel, with renovated wall arcading and early 'Decorated' tracery, is somewhat later; its stone vault was put up by Lord Grimthorpe.

The stone choir screen of about 1380 survives, but the bishop's throne and choir stalls are late Victorian. The sanctuary's principal adornments are the richly traceried and tabernacled chantries of Abbots Wallingford and Ramryge, and the splendid reredos of 1484 with its canopied niches and modern

statues. There are several good brasses, including some of monks and the rectangular plate, in the Flemish manner, to Abbot de la Mare (d. 1375). Some portions of St. Alban's shrine have been pieced together in the retro-choir; flanking it are the wooden watching loft and the ornate Perpendicular chantry of Humphrey, Duke of Gloucester (d. 1447).

Alone of our cathedrals, and a relic of its parish church days, St. Alban's has a Jacobean bread cupboard. It was used within recent years, and I once found the cathedral agreeably redolent of new bread.

82   In the presbytery: chantries and the altarpiece

Salisbury

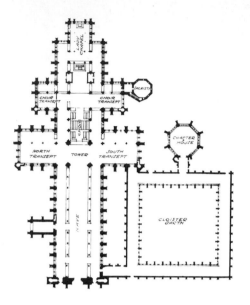

The last of England's pre-Reformation cathedrals established on its present site, Salisbury served a diocese with a complicated earlier history. The two Wessex bishoprics of Sherborne and Ramsbury were both held, from 1058, by the 'Lotharingian' Herman who had been a chaplain to King Edward the Confessor. After the Norman Conquest the two sees were formally united, the headquarters being moved to the fortified hill of Old Sarum. A new cathedral, with Rhenish flanking towers, was started by Herman and finished by St. Osmund. Fine, ornately Romanesque extensions were made in the twelfth century (see p. 25).

Disputes eventually arose, in a somewhat confined area containing both a cathedral and an important castle, between the garrison and the secular clergy who served the cathedral. About 1217, when Bishop Richard Poore became bishop, things came to a head, and he decided to move the whole cathedral establishment down to an empty site, in the Avon valley, near the village of Milford. Work started, in 1220, on the one English Gothic cathedral designed as a new, and in plan a complete building, with no previous church to complicate its design. The main fabric was nearly complete by 1258.

The new cathedral's basic plan included the elements—a long nave, two pairs of transepts giving space for several side altars, a square-ended presbytery, and an eastern Lady Chapel, then thought desirable in any great English

83   In the nave: diagonal view

84   In the Lady Chapel

Gothic church. Though its internal height is 81 feet, a good deal more than in such cathedrals as Wells, Lincoln, and Lichfield, its interior was far lower than its great apsidal opposite numbers in France. Its ground plan remained almost unchanged, and the late Perpendicular chapels which later flanked the Lady Chapel were trimmed away by Wyatt who also demolished the separate belfry.

The Lady Chapel was built first, and elements in its design, particularly a three-aisled plan and the slimness of its Purbeck marble columns, mark it off from the rest of the cathedral. Most of the church is a copybook rendering of one version of Early English, with creamy Chilmark stone varied by dark marble shafts and piers, with simple vaulting and sparing ornament. But dogtooth decoration edges the choir and transept arches, and the carving on label stops is richer in the slightly later nave. Yet the entire effect is more austere than one finds at Wells, in the nave at Lincoln, or at Ely. Nearly all the windows are lancets, but plate tracery appears in the four transepts, and the triforium openings anticipate the Geometrical idiom.

Salisbury's main glory, and some features caused by its erection, are later than 1300. The tower and spire—England's highest surviving steeple, are early 'Decorated', and the flying buttresses and external and interior struts

85   Monument to Lord Wyndham (d. 1745) by Rysbrack

which support the extra weight put on the crossing piers are of the early fourteenth century. So too are the inverted arches across the eastern transepts, while across the western transepts the two magnificent girder arches are of about 1460.

The cathedral is pitifully poor in mediaeval furnishings, and as little old glass is left a cold feeling goes with its severe architectural perfection. Its tombs and monuments form a magnificent collection; those in the nave are not, thanks to Wyatt's tidying up, in their original positions. The tomb of Bishop Giles of Bridport (d. 1262) is specially fine, Bishop Wyvil's brass (c. 1375) is unusually interesting, and the lovely Perpendicular chantry of Bishop Audley (d. 1524) took the place, after his translation, of one at Hereford. The Renaissance monuments of the Earl of Hertford (d. 1621) and Sir Thomas Gorges (erected 1635) are the most imposing of a large post-Reformation group.

The cloisters, and the splendid octagonal Chapter House with its richly sculptured arcading, are a little later than the main fabric. The Close, with its houses of various dates, is the most famous of all such cathedral precincts. It was when he was 'wandering . . . round the purlieus of Salisbury Cathedral' that Trollope conceived the story of his first Barsetshire novel, and Salisbury resembles 'Barchester' more closely than do other cathedral cities. But Trollope's references to its *towered* cathedral cannot be reconciled with this cathedral's architecture.

Southwark

Like St. Alban's cathedral, Southwark is a one-time monastic church which gained cathedral status after a long spell as a parish church. From soon after 1100 the Augustinian priory church of St. Mary Overy flourished near the southern end of London Bridge. Remains of the Norman church are in the nave and North transept of the present building. The Bishops of Winchester had a mansion in Southwark which long lay in their diocese, and much of what one now sees in the fabric is due to their interest. After the Dissolution the priory church became St. Saviour's parish church. By the 1830's it was in decay, and its old nave was replaced in early Victorian Gothic. Sir Arthur Blomfield's present nave was built in the 1890's, and when in 1905 the Southwark diocese was created the church became a cathedral.

Southwark's main glory lies in its simple Early English eastern limb. Started about 1206, with subtle differences between its two sides, and with the original bosses included in a renewed vault, it is excellent, square-ended lancet Gothic, so that at Southwark Londoners and tourists can get a better idea of English Gothic than they can from the essentially French Gothic of Westminster Abbey. The vaulted retrochoir, with a wealth of moulded decoration, a double arcade, and a set of beautifully furnished eastern chapels, is uniquely attractive; it lost a projecting chapel in the 1830's.

The South transept was built in the fourteenth century, but was repaired

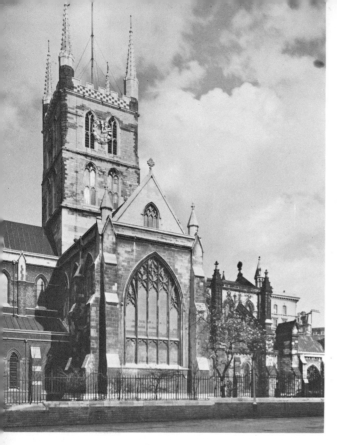

87 *Tower and transept, southern view*

88 *Nave, choir and altarpiece*

by Cardinal Beaufort, Bishop of Winchester. The pinnacled central tower is Perpendicular of the fifteenth century; here and elsewhere London grime has caused heavy restoration on the cathedral's external stonework. The church's finest late mediaeval treasure is the towering altarpiece, given about 1520 by Bishop Fox of Winchester and now decked out with modern statues; it is on the same lines as that in Winchester Cathedral. Near it, Bishop Lancelot Andrewes (d. 1626) is commemorated by a restored Carolean tomb. The modern choir fittings are by Blomfield and Bodley, while the High Altar and various other altars and fittings are by Comper.

The recessed and canopied tomb of the poet John Gower (d. 1408) is of fine quality, and the cathedral has other literary links. Shakespeare long lived in the parish, where the Globe Theatre was sited, his brother Edmund was buried in the church in 1607, and other Elizabethan dramatists, Fletcher and Massinger among them, were well known in the parish.

Among its other treasures Southwark Cathedral has some attractive mural monuments, and a splendid set of engraved floor slabs, mostly of the eighteenth century.

89　*In the retrochoir, early thirteenth century*

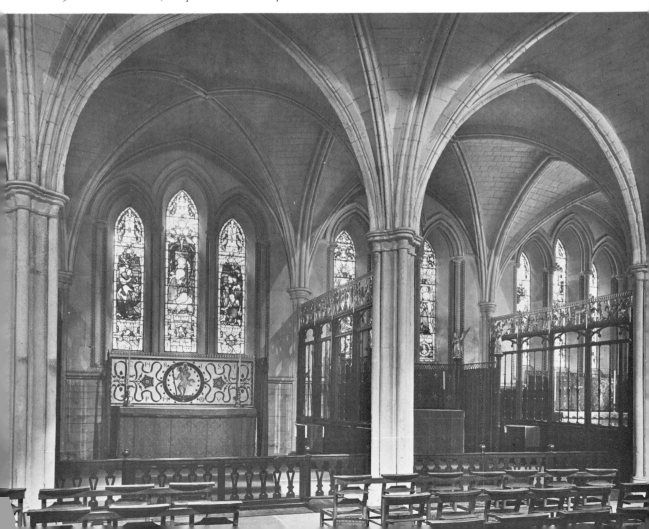

Southwell

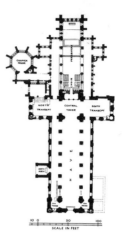

SCALE IN FEET

In the Middle Ages Southwell Minster was an important secular College in the diocese of York which then included Nottinghamshire. Its suppression had not fully been achieved when Mary I became Queen. She re-established the College which survived her death to continue in Elizabethan and later times. It was, however, dissolved under an Act of 1840. But when in 1884 an Anglican diocese was created to include Nottinghamshire and Derbyshire Southwell Minster became its cathedral.

A Saxon minster was replaced by an imposing Norman church whose nave, transepts, central tower and western towers (now with modern spires) remain as an outstanding achievement of severe Romanesque design. The transepts' inner walls have varied and interesting Norman treatment, while their gables have diaper decoration like some at Lincoln. Above the great rounded tower arches the tower's two ornamental stages place it high among England's surviving Norman towers; those at the West end are also excellent works of their kind. The imposing nave, with cylindrical columns, large triforium arches of a somewhat dominant character, and the unaltered clerestorey with its rows of round windows, is a little changed Romanesque achievement.

Southwell's choir limb is admirable Early English Gothic; like Ely Southwell is a cathedral half Romanesque and half Gothic, well showing the differ-

90 Norman exterior, Perpendicular West win

91   *In the Norman nave*

92   *The Early English choir*

ence between the two great mediaeval artistic traditions. Comparatively low, the choir has no triforium, but its deeply moulded arches, clustered columns, vaulting and vault shafts, and lancet windows make it a work of very high quality; as in some Augustinian churches the two eastern bays project unaisled.

The fourteenth-century designers gave Southwell Minster its choir screen and the comparatively small, polygonal Chapter House for which it is specially famed. The choir screen is most splendid; like the sacristy at Bristol it has some 'flying' vault ribs. The Chapter House and its vestibule comprise a fine 'Decorated' masterpiece, with sculptured detail including heads and, best known, naturalistic foliage unsurpassed in England.

142

Its West window apart, the Minster has little important Perpendicular work. The brass lectern of about 1500 came from Newstead Abbey, and in its sanctuary Southwell resembles Lichfield in having fine Continental glass (from Paris) of the early sixteenth century. Like the partly ruined archiepiscopal palace the tomb of the Elizabethan Archbishop Sandys (d. 1588) recalls the ancient York connection.

93　In the Chapter House; foliate capital, fourteenth century

Wells

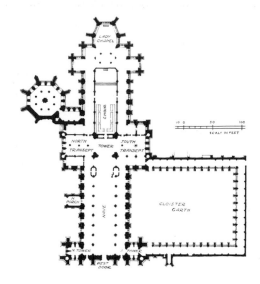

The Somerset diocese was separated from that of Sherborne in 909, with its headquarters placed at Wells. But the little town did not have an unbroken episcopal history. Despite the strengthening, by the Lorrainer Bishop Giso (1069–88) of its secular Chapter his successor John de Villula moved to Bath where he started a large new church for his Benedictine cathedral monastery. For most of the twelfth century Bath was Somerset's one cathedral city, and this had a restrictive effect on the architecture of the church at Wells. The work there of Bishop Robert of Lewes (1136–66) seems to have been no more than the repair and eastward lengthening of the Saxon church, and Wells seems never to have had a completely Norman cathedral.★ When, about 1190, the present Gothic cathedral was started it had a new site North of the older building. In 1244 the diocese settled down under its dual title of Bath and Wells, with two cathedrals of which that at Wells had a Dean and secular canons.

Of no great size, Wells is renowned for its architectural beauty, for the picturesqueness of its precincts, and for their unrivalled mediaeval character. The new cathedral was England's first of an almost wholly Gothic design. The Early English work in its transepts and nave is beautiful in the creamy hue of its Doulting stone (unvaried by dark marble shafts), in its clustered

★ See W. H. St.-J. Hope in *Archaeological Journal*, Vol. LXVII (1910).

94 *From the bishop's garden, the wells and their cathedral*

columns, richly varied foliate or figure capitals, and deeply moulded arches. The triforium arches are in continuous rows and, in a West of England manner, without capitals. The nave ends in the wide, impressive, but architecturally deceptive façade, important for its surviving thirteenth-century sculpture. The three western doorways are unimpressive, and the upper stages of the western towers are early Perpendicular.

The 'Decorated' additions to Wells Cathedral are of great distinction. As at Lichfield the Lady Chapel, an elongated octagon built soon after 1300, was first a separate building. But when the master mason William Joy lengthened and brilliantly transformed the choir limb he designed the most

145

exquisite of England's retrochoirs, and low-rise eastern transepts, like those at Hereford, to link the enlarged choir and the Lady Chapel. The central tower, the most beautiful tower of its period over any English cathedral, had already been built; its weight had to be sustained by unique, unattractive inverted arches across three of the earlier crossing arches.

By about 1400 the main fabric was complete. The stone choir screen, the misericords, and some splendid glass are of the fourteenth century, and the mediaeval tombs and chantries, mostly of bishops, are of great beauty. The cathedral was never important for the burials of leading Somerset laity, and its best post-Reformation monuments are also to bishops. The early Renaissance pulpit, of the 1540's, is important for English art as a whole.

The fourteenth-century octagonal Chapter House, above an earlier crypt, is of special beauty. The precincts are what make Wells a particularly loved cathedral city. The moated Palace, the Deanery as largely rebuilt in the fifteenth century, the Archdeaconry with its wheel window, the perfect collegiate grouping of Vicars' Close, and the varied houses of North Liberty combine to give a supremely Barchesterian impression.

96 *A choir transformed, thirteenth and fourteenth centuries*

Winchester

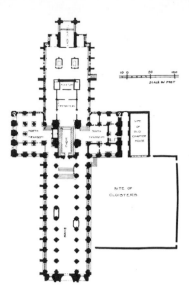

One of England's most historic cities, Winchester has been the seat of a bishop ever since the Wessex see was moved, about 679, from the Oxfordshire Dorchester. The boundaries of its diocese have varied, and its area has been diminished, but its status remained high and it was, in the Middle Ages and later, among the richest English bishoprics.

Mr. Martin Biddle's excavations have shown that the pre-Conquest cathedral (also the ceremonial worshipping place of the Wessex kings) was, by the eleventh century, an imposing building with a massive pair of western transepts; it lay North of the present cathedral. From the time of St. Ethelwold, bishop from 963 to 984, the cathedral was served by a large community of Benedictine monks.

The cathedral is still, in the main, the great Norman Romanesque building (once with a longer nave and two western towers) begun by Bishop Walkelin and his brother Simeon who was the cathedral prior. The crypt, below the presbytery and indicating the ground plan of the original East end, is part of this Norman church. The transepts, with wooden roofs and interesting outer aisles, are severe early Norman work, little altered when almost everything was Gothicised along the cathedral's main axis. The original tower fell in 1107 and its successor is still the squat one of the twelfth century; Mr. John Harvey has cogently suggested that it once had a spire.

148

The single-storey retrochoir, and the first bay of the Lady Chapel, are Early English additions of about 1200. The final portion of the Lady Chapel is late Perpendicular, making Winchester England's longest cathedral.

As at St. Alban's the presbytery was unimpressively recast, with a square East end, in the fourteenth century, but its present clerestorey and timber vault are late Perpendicular work by Thomas Bertie. Far more impressive was the gradual transformation, in some 50 years from about 1360, of the nave. The West front, and the nave's western extremity were newly built by Bishop Edington (1346–66) but the rest of the nave was recast, without total replacement, by Bishop William of Wykeham (1367–1404). The Norman pillars were cased with early Perpendicular stonework, the bold triforium stage was eliminated, and a new clerestorey and a magnificent lierne vault replaced the Norman upper structure; only in the eastern part of the North aisle can one see much of the severe early Norman work.

149

98 *Wykeham and Wynford's transformation: the nave*

99 *In the retrochoir: the Waynflete and Gardiner chantries*

Despite many changes, and the loss of nearly all its old glass, this great cathedral is still rich in contents and furnishings. As at Lincoln the sculptured font is a Romanesque importation in black Tournai marble. In the choir the early 'Decorated' canopied choir stalls are the oldest canopied set in England, while the great reredos given by Bishop Fox (1500–28) splendidly dominates the sanctuary. Bishop Fox's side screens support Renaissance chests containing the bones of Saxon kings and bishops. Jane Austen's simple floor slab apart, the mediaeval and post-Reformation monuments are of great interest and merit. The chantry chapels are the best group in the country, while the Renaissance or Georgian monuments include work by Le Sueur, Cheere, Flaxman and Chantrey.

150

100 *At Winchester: the South transept and the tower still display an essentially Nor character*

Worcester

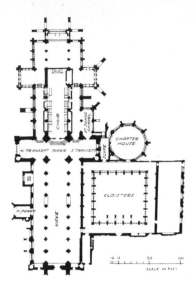

The diocese of Worcester was formed, about 680, from that of Lichfield, and the throne of its bishops remained, without interruption, in the same city. About 960 St. Oswald reorganised the cathedral's staffing so that it was served, until Henry VIII's reign, by Benedictine monks. The church was the most Gothicised monastic cathedral, and its priory buildings, including fine cloisters and England's only centrally planned Norman Chapter House, are fine and mostly well preserved. On its site above the Severn the cathedral is one of the most nobly sited in the country.

St. Wulstan, bishop from 1062 to 1095 and the last pre-Conquest bishop to remain in office, had not wished to replace the Saxon cathedral. But he felt that he must follow the prevalent trend, and the magnificent crypt of his time is the finest early Norman crypt in England and the best survival of the Romanesque cathedral. The basic masonry of the transepts and of the aisle walls in the nave, and some work at the West end of the choir limb, are also Norman.

The exterior stonework, much restored and altered all over the cathedral, gives no clue to the style of the nave's two western bays. These, with their blend of round and pointed arches, are excellent Transitional Norman work—among the best in England. The rest of the church's steady transformation, after St. Wulstan's canonisation in 1203, was in the various Gothic styles.

152

The eastern limb, with its fine, lofty Lady Chapel, a second pair of transepts, and a simply vaulted choir, is excellent Early English. The wall arcading, with its spandrel carvings, is a beautiful feature, and the choir has fine detail though, as at Canterbury and Rochester, the crypt causes an inadequate internal height. Most of the nave was rebuilt in a severe, though dignified 'Decorated' idiom, while an interruption caused by the Black Death did not affect the mainly 'Decorated' character of the later work on its southern side. But the splendid central tower, by John Clyve and built about 1375, is early Perpendicular.

Though the early sixteenth-century misericords remain, the other fittings in the choir are exceptionally ugly Victorian efforts, and some Hardman windows do little to redeem the generally poor Victorian glass. But the

153

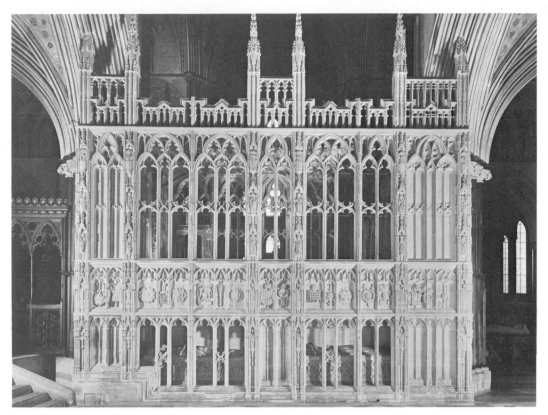

103   *The chantry of Prince Arthur*

cathedral is outstandingly rich in the variety and quality of its tombs and monuments. Two excellent Purbeck marble effigies commemorate Bishops William of Blois (d. 1236) and Walter de Cantilupe (d. 1266). Earlier, and an outstanding marble figure, is the effigy of King John, with his head between little figures of Saints Oswald and Wulstan. No less historic is the splendid Perpendicular chantry of Prince Arthur (d. 1502) whose survival to full manhood could have prevented the accession of Henry VIII. Elizabethan monuments apart, the seventeenth-century and Georgian memorials include work by local carvers and such 'national' sculptors as Stanton of Holborn, Nollekens, Wilton, the younger Bacon, and Chantrey, while Roubiliac's dramatic monument to Bishop Hough (d. 1743) is one of our finest Baroque memorials outside Westminster Abbey.

Splendid simplicity in Worcester's Norman crypt

York

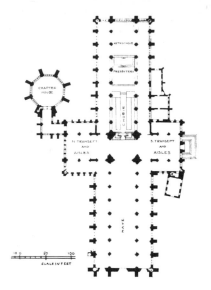

With its origins going back to St. Paulinus and King Edwin of Northumbria in 627 the northern archbishop's see of York is nearly as old and historic as that of Canterbury. The Minster's history as a cathedral has been unbroken, and it is close set in the most convincingly mediaeval English city. Though it was always served by a secular Chapter its precincts were less spacious than those of most other non-monastic cathedrals.

The successive Saxon cathedrals have disappeared. So too, bar the core of the crossing piers, has the somewhat unimpressive church built under the Normans. Even in the crypt the fine Transitional Norman pillars from the crypt of Archbishop Roger (d. 1181) are not in their first positions. The present Minster emerged from a long process of Gothic replacement, on massive lines and in various styles, from about 1220 to 1474. Its width, and an interior height great by English standards, make it one of our largest cathedrals.

Rebuilding started with the two transepts, each originally of four bays. The southern one is the earlier; at its South end a complex arrangement of arcading and windows includes a wheel window and contrasts with the simplicity of the equal-sized 'Five Sisters' lancets in the North transept. The nave, like the other parts of the Minster with a main vault of wood, was built just before and soon after 1300. It is of severe and distinguished dignity, and the way in which the mullions of its 'Decorated' clerestorey windows

156

104   North-eastern aspect, from the city wall

ran down through the triforium anticipated the Perpendicular style. The designer was Simon the mason; at the nave's western end more elaboration was allowed, so that the West front has fine panelling, three doorways and a notably splendid curvilinear West window.

The choir limb was built, between 1361 and about 1400, in a curious, not very attractive blend of 'Decorated' and 'Perpendicular'. As in the nave the arcade spandrels contain shields of arms, while the two little transepts, not projecting beyond the aisle walls, were built so that their tall windows could light the sanctuary. The eastern façade is most effective, and its great Perpendicular window is almost the largest in England. The Minster's three-towered silhouette was completed at various fifteenth-century dates; to save weight the builders omitted the pinnacles planned for the central tower.

The splendid stone choir screen, with canopied niches and original statues, is of the late fifteenth century. Nearly all the original choir stalls were burnt

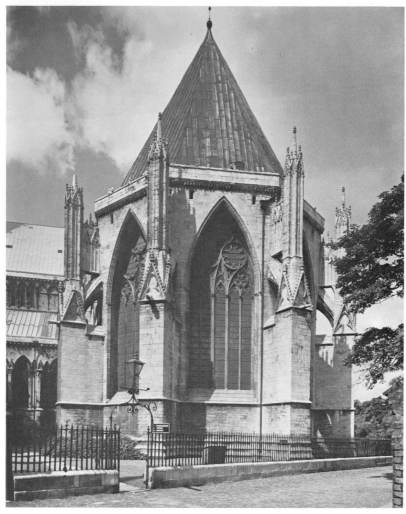

in 1829, but were soon replaced by the convincingly Gothic stalls which, along with more typically Georgian pewing, now furnish the choir. The early 'Decorated' octagonal Chapter House is remarkable because its roof is supported without a central pier; as at Southwell its wall arcading has beautiful naturalistic foliage.

Its glass is the supreme glory of York Minster. Alone of England's cathedrals it has kept nearly all its mediaeval glazing, and it is easily the best cathedral in

York: an interior scene and the great East window

the country for this aspect of the art of the Middle Ages. The thirteenth-century grisaille glass in the Five Sisters lancets, the fourteenth-century glass in the nave, and the great expanses of early fifteenth-century glazing in the East window and in the eastern transepts are all of great merit, while eighteenth-century windows by the local glazier Peckitt add variety to the collection. The Minster's mediaeval tombs and post-Reformation monuments are also of beauty and interest. Local laity and county magnates are commemorated along with archbishops, other clergy, and one of Edward III's sons who died as a boy and was buried in the church where his parents had been married. The Renaissance, Baroque, and Georgian monuments include Gibbons' figure of Archbishop Lamplugh (d. 1691), and excellent sculpture by Nost and by Guelfi of Bologna.

107   *The tomb of Archbishop Sterne, d. 1683*